How Do You Know?

A Dialogue

How Do You Know?

A Dialogue

Gordon Barnes

Hackett Publishing Company, Inc.
Indianapolis/Cambridge

Copyright © 2021 by Hackett Publishing Company, Inc.

24 23 22 21   1 2 3 4 5 6 7

For further information, please address
    Hackett Publishing Company, Inc.
    P.O. Box 44937
    Indianapolis, Indiana 46244-0937

    www.hackettpublishing.com

Cover and interior design by E. L. Wilson
Composition by Aptara, Inc.

Cataloging-in-Publication data can be accessed via the Library of Congress
Online Catalog.
Library of Congress Control Number: 2021932233

ISBN-13: 978-1-62466-991-0 (pbk.)
ISBN-13: 978-1-62466-993-4 (PDF ebook)

Contents

For Marnie

Acknowledgments

At its best, philosophy is a good conversation. I grew up in a family that loved good conversation, and no one has taught me more than the people I grew up with: Ellen Dodrill, Brenda Thompson, Martha Jones, Robert Barnes, and Laura Harris. Thanks to his great generosity, my brother Bob and I have had great conversations in places like London, Paris, Barcelona, and Madrid. In recent years, I have enjoyed great conversations with my brother-from-another-mother Joe Thompson. In philosophy, I have had three great conversation partners: Matt Davidson, John Kronen, and Joseph Long. I have learned more from them than I could ever recount. Since moving to Rochester, New York, I have enjoyed good conversations with Peter Karpien and Greg Garvey. My wife and I have enjoyed countless conversations around the dinner table with the Liebert family: David and Nancy; Peter and Amy; Tim and Natalie; Heidi, Dave, Abby, and Sarah. One of the best conversationalists I have ever met is Chuck Vanduzee. I could talk to Chuck from dawn to dusk and I sometimes have. Over the last sixteen years, I have had the pleasure of teaching philosophy at SUNY Brockport, and my time there has been filled with great conversations with students. There are too many of them to name here, but I am grateful to every one of them. In a telephone conversation with my editor Jeff Dean, he impressed on me that we live in an age in which knowledge is contested. Throughout this process, Jeff has given me great advice and support. I would never have gotten this done without the constant help and support of our respite workers, and dear friends—Tess Cooper, Ashley Samuels, and Bridget Behan. Finally, and most importantly, I am deeply grateful to my wife, Marnie Barnes. Over the last year, when our lives were more difficult than usual, she moved mountains to help me get this done. She read and commented on the entire manuscript and saved me from many mistakes. She is also my favorite conversation partner in the world.

Preface

This book is about problems of knowledge that arise in everyday life. If you are not an expert, then how can you know that another person is an expert? What if the experts are politically biased? Should you still trust them? More generally, what attitude should you take to the testimony of other people? Should you treat all testimony as "innocent until proven guilty," or is that just gullible? Does the internet make us better knowers, or is it really just a minefield of misinformation? Is it always irrational to believe a conspiracy theory? Suppose you find out that someone who is just as intelligent and well informed as you disagrees with you about something. How should that affect your belief? Should you change your mind or be less confident that you are right? Is it possible to know what is morally right and morally wrong? Is morality something that can be known? These are the questions that are discussed in this book. These issues are fundamentally *social*. Testimony, trust, and disagreement are in all relations between two or more people. Therefore I have chosen to write in the form of a dialogue. This is a dialogue between three college students—Paul, Steve, and Maya. Paul and Steve grew up together in a small town, and then they went off to college together. Over the course of their first year in college, Steve changed his mind about many things, but Paul did not. This was largely due to the fact that Steve trusted his professors, whereas Paul did not. Steve sees his professors as experts who tell the truth about the world, whereas Paul sees his professors as biased activists who want to indoctrinate him. So the friendship between Paul and Steve has started to fall apart. The third student in the dialogue, Maya, is a senior who offers to mediate a conversation between Paul and Steve to see if they can work out their differences. Their conversation takes them through all of the topics listed above. This is not a rhetorical exercise. These are difficult questions, and there are no easy answers. In Chapter One, they discuss whether it is possible for a non-expert to know if someone else is really an expert. This leads them to the question of when you should trust the testimony of another person. In Chapter Two, they discuss the reality and relevance of bias—both to trust in others and to trust in oneself. In Chapter Three, they discuss the internet and how it has affected us as knowers. This leads them to a discussion of conspiracy theories. In Chapter Four, they discuss the issue of disagreement between equally intelligent, well-informed people. Finally, in Chapter Five, they discuss the problem of moral knowledge. A paradox that reappears throughout the dialogue is that social trust is epistemologically problematic, yet it appears to be indispensable for the pursuit of knowledge by creatures like us.

Chapter One

Where Are the Experts?

Maya sits alone in her dorm room, trying to study. Across the hall, Paul and Steve are arguing loudly.

Paul: My mother told me herself, Steve! Don't call my mother a liar!

Steve: I'm not calling anyone a liar, Paul. I'm just saying that I know your mother is wrong.

Paul: You don't know that!

Steve: Yes, I do!

Paul: No, you don't! You're being a jerk!

Unable to study, Maya gets up from her desk and walks across the hall.

Maya: Guys, you're getting pretty loud. Can you dial it down?

Paul: Sorry, Maya.

Maya: What's going on? What are you fighting about?

Paul: My brother is autistic.

Maya: Yes, I know. I have a cousin who's autistic. We talked about it last fall.

Paul: Oh yeah, I guess I forgot about that. Well, I'm not surprised. The percentage of people with autism has been increasing steadily for years now. And you have to wonder why that is.

Steve: That's what we're fighting about.

Maya: Ohhh. Is this about vaccines?

Steve: You guessed it!

Paul: Look, before you call me an idiot . . .

Maya: I wasn't going to call you anything, Paul. I wouldn't do that.

Paul: Well, you're a better friend than Steve, then.

Steve: Give me a break.

Maya: Hold on, Steve. Go ahead, Paul. I'm listening.

Paul: My brother was completely typical when he was born, and he continued to be typical for nineteen months. He walked and talked and met all the developmental milestones. Then, at nineteen months, he got the MMR vaccine. And that's when he changed. Before the vaccine, one of his favorite things to do was to watch mom vacuum. After the vaccine, he would run away from the vacuum in terror and cover his ears. Before the vaccine, he was never bothered by any loud noises. After the vaccine, he would cover his ears at the slightest noise. He changed completely after the vaccine. My mother watched it with her own eyes. There is no way that was a coincidence. The MMR vaccine caused my brother's autism. People who deny that just aren't listening to the mothers who watch it happen. And that makes me angry.

Maya: I can understand that. But Paul, the idea that vaccines cause autism was based on a study that turned out to be fraudulent. In 1998, a man named Andrew Wakefield published a study in *The Lancet* in which he claimed that the measles-mumps-rubella vaccine (the MMR vaccine) caused autism in eleven children. But on closer inspection, researchers discovered that the study was a complete fraud. Wakefield's data were bogus. So this whole idea was based on fraud.

Paul: Yeah, I know about that. But that isn't why people like my mother believe that vaccines cause autism. They believe it because they see it with their own eyes. Parent after parent has reported this experience, but the experts just call them idiots. And as for the reaction to Wakefield, it wouldn't be the first time that the medical community refused to recognize something like this.

Maya: What do you mean?

Paul: In 1956, a woman named Alice Stewart published a survey of children who had died of cancer. The survey showed that just one X-ray of an unborn infant doubled their risk of getting cancer as a child. But it took twenty-four years for the US medical associations to accept that. In the meantime, her peers completely rejected her claims. One radiobiologist called her "senile." So it took the medical community twenty-four years to accept the fact that prenatal X-rays cause childhood cancer. So you'll forgive me if I don't completely trust them.

Steve: But that's just one case, Paul. You shouldn't base your opinion of all of medicine on just one case like that. And eventually the medical community figured it out. It took a while, sure, but they eventually got it right. It's now been over twenty years since the Wakefield study, and there have been no more studies that support it.

Paul: But it isn't just that. Like I said, parent after parent has observed their children develop symptoms of autism right after getting the vaccine.

Steve: I'm not denying that, Paul. But that doesn't show that the vaccine causes autism.

Paul: Are you saying it's just a coincidence?!

Steve: Yes, that's right. I know it's hard to believe it, but it is. It's just the result of timing. The MMR vaccine is given to children at around fifteen months, and the symptoms of autism start to appear between then and eighteen months. But it's just a coincidence.

Paul: Well, why do you think it's just a coincidence?

Steve: There are now lots of studies that have found no causal connection between the MMR vaccine and autism.

Paul: I don't think they've shown that.

Steve: Yes, they have. There are a whole bunch of studies that found no connection between vaccines and autism. They designed those studies to test exactly this question, and in study after study, they found no connection between vaccines and autism.

Paul: Well, that's a bad argument. Not finding that there *is* a connection is not the same thing as finding that *there is no connection*. The fact that they didn't find it doesn't mean that it isn't there.

Maya: There's actually a good phrase for that: *absence of evidence is not evidence of absence.*

Paul: Exactly!

Maya: Unfortunately, it isn't always true. In some circumstances, if you look for something and you don't find it, then that *is* evidence that it isn't there. For example, if I look in my closet for a gorilla, and I don't see a gorilla, then that really *is* evidence that there is no gorilla in my closet. That's because if there *were* a gorilla in my closet, then I would see it. So the fact that I don't see it is good evidence that there is no gorilla in my closet.

Steve: Exactly. And if there were a connection between vaccines and autism, then surely one of these studies that looked for a connection would have found one. But they didn't find any connection. So we have good reason to believe that there isn't one.

Paul: That is assuming that if there is a connection, then one of those studies would have found it. But here's my other problem with those studies: Most of the people in wealthy nations, where all these studies were done, have been vaccinated. So how can they compare rates of autism between people who were vaccinated and people who were not vaccinated when everyone has been vaccinated?

Maya: Not everyone in wealthy countries has been vaccinated. Some people, in various religious communities, don't get vaccinated.

Paul: True. But then how do we know that there isn't something *else* that causes autism in those communities?

Steve: That would be quite a coincidence.

Maya: Look, there was actually a study in Denmark that compared people who had been vaccinated with people who had not been vaccinated, and the rate of autism in both groups was almost exactly the same.

Paul: One study! Just one! Why would you trust that study instead of trusting all the mothers of autistic children who say that the MMR vaccine caused their child's autism?

Steve: I trust the experts who did the study because they are trained professionals who know what they're doing.

Paul: But you can't trust them on this!

Maya: Why not?

Paul: Because they're biased!

Maya: How are they biased?

Paul: They say it all the time: "If people stop getting vaccinated, then all sorts of horrible diseases will start coming back, and it will be disastrous for everyone." They say it repeatedly.

Maya: Well, that's true, isn't it?

Paul: Yes, but that's why you can't trust them on this. Look, they are very concerned that people will stop getting their kids vaccinated, and I get that. But that means that they have a vested interest in showing that vaccines are safe. So they have an ulterior motive for telling everyone that vaccines are safe. That's why I don't trust them. They would say that vaccines are safe, even if they weren't, just to keep everyone getting vaccinated.

Steve: That's a conspiracy theory.

Paul: No, it isn't. Like I said, they come right out and say as much— that they want everyone to keep getting vaccinated.

Steve: That doesn't mean they would lie about it.

Paul: How do you know that?

Steve: Because they are good people who know what they're doing!

Paul: That's so gullible. You're such a sheep.

Steve: Oh please! Here we go again!

Maya: What do you mean?

Steve: This is where we always wind up these days.

Paul: Yeah, that's about right.

Maya: I was wondering about that. When you guys came here last fall, you were really good friends. I don't think I ever saw one of you without the other one. Then I started to hear you fighting all the time. What happened?

Steve: Paul and I grew up together, in the same small town. When we came here for college, we were close friends. We did everything together—we liked the same things and the same people. Thinking back, we saw almost everything the same way. We almost never disagreed. But then I took some classes that got me thinking about things. I started to see things differently. Since then, I've changed my mind about almost everything. But that didn't happen to Paul. He stayed the same. And that's when we started fighting all the time.

Maya: Is that right Paul? Is that what happened?

Paul: I'll tell you what happened. Steve was completely brainwashed. That's what happened. All of a sudden, everything we were taught growing up was false, and everyone we knew was evil. And it all happened so fast, I just couldn't believe it. Steve was literally indoctrinated overnight. He needs to be de-programmed.

Steve: No, Paul, that's not what happened. What happened is that I listened to the *experts*—people who know a lot more than I do. I was open-minded enough to listen to them, learn from them. But you were too closed-minded for that, so you didn't learn anything.

Paul: Oh please. Give me a break. Those people aren't experts. They're biased and they're dogmatic, and they think they know a lot more than they do.

Steve: No, Paul. They're experts. I know that.

Paul: No, you don't know that, because it's impossible to know that.

Maya: Wait, what?

Paul: It's impossible for Steve to know that our professors are experts.

Maya: I don't understand. Why is that impossible?

Paul: In order to know that someone else is an expert, you would have to be an expert yourself. But Steve is not an expert. So Steve can't know if any of them are really experts.

Steve: That doesn't make any sense.

Paul: Yes, it does. I can prove it.

Steve: That's ridiculous.

Maya: Whoa! Hold on! To be fair, we need to hear this out. Go on Paul.

Paul: An expert is someone who knows a lot more in a particular area than most people do. That means that they have many true beliefs in that area, and they have relatively few false beliefs in that area.

Maya: That seems right.

Paul: Okay, so here is my argument. To be an expert is to have many true beliefs in an area, and few false beliefs in that area. So in order to know that someone is an expert, you would have to know that most of her beliefs in that area are true. But if you know that most of her beliefs in that area are true, *then you are already an expert in that area yourself*, since you know as much as an expert knows in that area. So, in order to know that someone is an expert, you would have to be an expert yourself. In most areas, none of us here is an expert, so none of us can know who the experts are or even if there are any experts at all.

Steve: That can't be right.

Maya: Hold on, Steve. We should think about this. Paul's argument deserves a response. If we think that non-experts can know that other people are experts, then we need to explain how we can know this. And in order to do that, we need to show that there is something wrong with Paul's argument.

Paul: Thank you. I appreciate that.

Steve: I think we can know who the experts are without being experts ourselves.

Paul: How can we know that?

Steve: Experts give evidence for their beliefs. We can examine that evidence for ourselves, and determine whether or not it is good evidence. You can do this over and over again, and if a person usually gives good evidence for her conclusions, then you have good reason to believe that she is an expert.

Paul: In some cases, that might work. But in a whole lot of cases, it won't work.

Steve: Why not?

Paul: It won't work, because in order to evaluate the evidence that the experts give, you also have to be an expert. Just think about research in economics, for example. Suppose that I want to know if the evidence that an economist gives for a particular claim is good evidence. What do I need to know in order to evaluate that evidence? I need to know what counts as good research in economics. And in order to know that, I need to understand the concepts and methods that are used in economics. I need to know exactly what is required for a study or an experiment in economics to produce results that are reliable. The more you think about it, you will see that in order to evaluate the evidence that is offered by an economist, you will need to know an awful lot about economics. You will need to be an economist, or something pretty close to it, yourself. And the same point applies to research in other areas too. In order to evaluate the evidence that is offered by experts, you need to be an expert yourself, or pretty close to it. So, if you are not an expert, you can never really know if the alleged experts have been offering good evidence for their claims or not.

Steve: Even if that is true in some areas, it isn't true in all areas. In some areas, even a non-expert can read the evidence and understand it just fine.

Paul: I disagree. Just think about the recent "replication crisis" in psychology.

Steve: What are you talking about?

Paul: In 2015, a group of psychologists published a report in the journal *Science*, in which they reported that 270 psychologists repeated one hundred previously published experiments in psychology, and they got the same results *in only 40 percent of the experiments*. In other words, they failed to replicate the results of 60 percent of the experiments. Many of these experiments in psychology were taken to be reliable experiments. People in psychology assumed that the results of the experiments were trustworthy. But when these psychologists conducted the experiments again, they got different results 60 percent of the time. Since then, there have been many more failures to replicate the results of experiments in psychology. That's why some people are calling it a crisis. The methods used in the discipline, which were assumed to be reliable, now appear to be unreliable.

Maya: That's not quite right. What happened is that some people in psychology started using some very questionable research practices.

Paul: What do you mean?

Maya: In some cases, here is what they did. They performed an experiment a large number of times—like twenty times, and in eighteen of those experiments there was no significant result. But in the other two, there was a significant result. So they would publish one of those two experiments and put the other nineteen in a drawer somewhere. People would be impressed by the significant result of the published experiment, but that's just because they were unaware of the other eighteen experiments that found no significant result.

Steve: Wow. That's awful.

Maya: Yes, I think it is. It was bad science.

Paul: Well, suppose that's true. It doesn't contradict my point.

Steve: What is your point?

Paul: The evidence that was originally offered by these psychologists was not good evidence. But only a professional in psychology could figure that out. No one else could tell that these experiments were really weak evidence. And the same point applies to other areas of expertise. If you are not an expert in an area, then you cannot tell whether or not the research in that area is reliable. Steve claimed that we could know that someone was an expert by evaluating the evidence that they offer and seeing that it's good evidence. My point is that in many cases, we cannot do that without being experts ourselves.

Steve: Okay, I see your point. But we have other reasons to believe that some people are experts and that they are generally reliable.

Paul: What reasons?

Steve: Experts have credentials. If someone has a PhD in her field, and she has published in the very best journals in her field, and all of her peers in the discipline say that she is an expert, then we have good reason to believe that she is an expert.

Paul: I don't think that's a good reason.

Steve: Why not?

Paul: Those "credentials" are just the opinions of more people who claim to be experts. When someone gets a degree, like a PhD, that is nothing more than a group of people saying: "This person is an expert." But why should I believe the people who are saying that?

Steve: Because they're experts!

Paul: But you were supposed to be giving me a reason to believe that someone else is an expert. I ask you how you know that someone is an expert and you tell me to trust the testimony of other people, who say that these people are experts. I ask you why I should trust their testimony and you tell me that I should trust them *because they're experts*! You're just assuming that the people granting the PhDs and editing the professional journals are experts. But that is exactly what you cannot know. You have assumed what you were supposed to be proving.

Steve: You are impossible.

Maya: I think I can help here. Paul is saying that this argument for trusting experts is *circular*.

Steve: What do you mean?

Maya: A circular argument is an argument that assumes what it is supposed to prove.

Steve: But my argument doesn't do that. I'm trying to prove that our professors are experts. My evidence is that many *other* people— the people who gave them their degrees and published their books and articles—have said that they are experts. I am assuming that those *other* people are trustworthy because *they* are experts. My argument does not assume that the professors at our college are experts. So my argument is not circular.

Maya: Strictly speaking, that's true. But your argument does assume that certain people are experts—the people who conferred the degrees and published the books and articles. But how do we know that those people are experts? Paul has argued that we, who are not experts, cannot know that *anyone* else is an expert. Your argument assumes that someone else, at another university or publishing company, is an expert. So you are assuming exactly the sort of thing that Paul says we cannot know.

Steve: Yes, I see what you mean. But why would all these people say that our professors are experts if they're not? The fact that all these people agree that our professors are experts seems like a good reason to believe it.

Paul: No, I don't think so. The mere fact that a bunch of people agree that someone is an expert is not a good reason to believe that they are an expert. The members of a cult all agree that their leader is an expert in spiritual matters. If your argument is a good argument, then we should believe that the leader of every cult is really an expert in all spiritual matters. But obviously we shouldn't believe that.

Steve: Oh *please*! Are you really comparing universities to cults?!

Paul: No, not exactly. But there is such a thing as *group-think*, and even very smart people are susceptible to it. People who study together and socialize together and have a vested interest in seeing themselves as experts are likely to see each other as experts, even if they really aren't. That is especially true when their incomes and their social status depend on it. But it isn't conscious or deliberate. It's a kind of self-deception that happens all the time. People tell themselves that they know things even when they don't. People do this all the time, and the so-called experts are just particularly good at it. So here is an explanation of all this agreement amongst the "experts"—they are under the spell of a kind of group-think. We already know that this sort of thing happens all the time. So that seems to me to be just as good an explanation as the idea that they really are experts.

Steve: Do you really think that? You think that college professors are all just deceiving themselves?

Paul: I think there's no way to *know* whether or not they are. If you're not an expert yourself, then it's impossible for you to tell whether the people who claim to be experts are really experts or just all think alike.

Steve: Why not *trust* them? These people—a very large group of people—say that they are experts. I think you should *trust* them, at least initially. You should give them the benefit of the doubt.

Paul: That's so *gullible*. It's a sure way to get conned.

Steve: It requires you to take a risk. That's true. But I think it's rational to take that risk. It's rational to trust them, at least to start with.

Paul: How could it be rational to trust them? I don't even know those people.

Steve: It's rational to trust them because trust is necessary for any learning whatsoever. Without trusting other people, we could not know most of what we know. Think about it. Most of the things that you know today are things that you learned from someone else. Think about all the things you know about foreign countries that you have never visited. How do you know those things? You had to learn them from someone else. And in order to do that, you had to *trust* those people—trust that they were telling the truth. Think about everything you know about the history of the world before you were born. You didn't witness any of those things. So how do you know about them? You learned them from other people—people who witnessed them and wrote them down. And again—you had to trust those people in order to learn all that history. All the things that you have learned from reading books and magazines and watching television—they were all learned from other people. And in order to learn all those things from those people, you had to *trust* them. Without trust, you would not have learned most of what you have learned in your life. So it's rational to trust people because that's how you learn and gain knowledge. And that's why you should trust the experts when they say that they are experts.

Paul: When you're a child, you trust people because you really have no choice. But I don't think you *know* that people are trustworthy. You just have to trust them anyway. But that's because you're a child. Once you become an adult, you should be more cautious about who you trust. Through your own experience, you find out who is trustworthy and who is not. And so you acquire *evidence* for the trustworthiness of the people you know. You also get evidence that certain people, in certain situations tend to be trustworthy. From then on, you have good reason to trust people like that, in situations like that. But you should never trust anyone without having that kind of evidence—evidence that they are the type of person who is trustworthy, or that this is the type of situation in which people tend to be trustworthy. Only when you have a track record of reliability like that should you trust people. My professors at college have no such track record, at least not with me. So my reasons for trusting some people do not extend to my professors or any other so-called experts.

Maya: I think I can help here. Steve thinks that testimony is a basic source of knowledge, whereas Paul denies that.

Paul: You lost me there. What does that mean?

Maya: This will take a minute to explain. I learned about it in one of my philosophy classes last semester.

Paul: That's okay. I think we're at an impasse, so let's give it a try.

Maya: A basic source of knowledge is a source that does not depend on any *other* source of knowledge in order to be trustworthy. When you get information from a basic source of knowledge, then you can trust that information unless you have a specific reason not to trust it. When you get information from a basic source of knowledge, you don't have to prove that the information is correct in order to trust it. The fact that it came from a basic source of knowledge is good reason to trust it.

Paul: Can you give an example?

Maya: Yes. Sense perception is a basic source of knowledge. Let's just focus on vision. If you see a tree in front of you, then you should believe that there is a tree in front of you, unless you have some specific reason to doubt it. The fact that you see the tree is good reason to believe that there is a tree there.

Paul: Seeing is believing.

Maya: That's right. And seeing is *knowing* too. When you see the tree, you know that it's there. If I asked you: "How do you know that there is a tree there?" You would be right to say: "Because I *see* it." That is just what it means to say that vision is a basic source of knowledge. Seeing something is a source of knowledge that does not depend on any other source of knowledge. When you see a tree, you know that there is a tree there, and you don't need any other evidence or argument for that.

Paul: But you could be mistaken, right? Your eyes might be playing tricks on you. Maybe you are hallucinating.

Maya: Yes, that's right. Vision is fallible. But that doesn't prevent it from being a basic source of knowledge. This is really just common sense, if you think about it. You just noted that when you see something, you might be hallucinating. So are you going to stop trusting your eyes? *Should* you stop trusting your own eyes?

Paul: No, I don't think so.

Maya: Exactly. As long as your vision is *generally reliable*—it gets things right most of the time, you are right to trust your own eyes. You don't need to prove that your vision is accurate in order to trust it. And as long as your eyes are working, you can get knowledge through them.

Steve: Don't some people deny that?

Maya: Yes. In philosophy, they are called "skeptics." They deny that we know anything. But I assume that none of us here is really a skeptic.

Paul: Well, that's a much larger issue, so let's set it aside for now. I'm happy to agree, at least for the sake of argument, that vision is a basic source of knowledge. But what does any of that have to do with experts and testimony?

Maya: Well, Steve is saying that testimony is also a basic source of knowledge. If someone knows something, and they tell it to you, then you know it too.

Paul: Wait a minute! You just snuck a lot in there. In your description of that situation, you just assumed that the person giving testimony had knowledge and that they were saying something true. But how do we, the listeners, *know* that what they said is true?

Maya: Well, if testimony is a basic source of knowledge, then if someone tells you something, that they know to be true, then through their testimony, you also come to know that it's true.

Steve: Yeah, I agree with that. It's sort of like seeing through someone else's eyes. They came to know it for themselves, and now, by telling you, they give their knowledge to you.

Paul: But you're still not answering my question. How do you know that the person giving the testimony is telling the truth? You keep saying that *if* what they say is true, then I know it's true. But that doesn't answer my question. How do *I* know that it's true?

Maya: I understand your question, but you're forgetting what it means to say that a source of knowledge is *basic*. Remember, to say that a source of knowledge is basic is to say that it does not need any independent proof or evidence to be trustworthy. When you ask: "How do I know that the person giving the testimony is telling the truth?" you are asking for some proof or evidence that testimony should be trusted. But if testimony is a basic source of knowledge, then it doesn't need any independent proof or evidence in order to be trusted.

Paul: This seems like a shell game.

Maya: Suppose that you see a tree in the front yard, and by seeing it, you know that there is a tree there. If I ask you: "Yeah, but how do you *know* that there's really a tree there?" You should say: "Because I see it." In the same way, if you ask me: "How do you know that a water molecule contains two atoms of Hydrogen?" I will say: "Because my chemistry professor told me so." And that is just as good an answer as the first one.

Paul: But not everyone tells the truth. People lie all the time. They also make honest mistakes and say things that are false. So people often say things that are false.

Maya: Yes, testimony is fallible. But so is vision. Remember, your eyes can play tricks on you. A stick submerged in water can look bent, even though it is really straight. Vision is also fallible. But unless we are ready to become skeptics, and doubt our own eyes, that should not lead us to stop trusting vision. As long as our vision is generally reliable, that is enough to trust it, without having to prove its reliability every time. And the same goes for testimony. It is fallible, but it is generally trustworthy. That is enough for it to qualify as a basic source of knowledge.

Paul: Okay, fair enough. Fallibility alone does not disqualify testimony from being a basic source of knowledge. But I'm still not convinced that testimony *is* a basic source of knowledge. Why should I think that?

Maya: Well, remember that Steve gave an argument for his view, and it was actually a lot like the argument for taking vision as a basic source of knowledge. The argument goes like this. A whole lot of the things that you think you know are based on the testimony of other people. If you think about it, it's probably most of what you take yourself to know. And if you think about all the sources from which you got all that information, you did not have independent evidence that they were reliable sources. So if you need proof of reliability for every source that you trust, in order to acquire knowledge from them, then you do not know most of the things that you think you know.

Paul: Okay, sure. Then I don't really know any of those things.

Maya: You don't know that there is a Great Wall in China? You don't know that George Washington was the first president of the United States? You don't know that there are poisonous snakes in Australia? You don't know that . . .

Paul: Okay, okay. I get the point. I learned all those things from the testimony of other people. That's true. But I learned those things from my teachers when I was growing up, and my teachers had a track record of getting things right—one that I could confirm for myself. So I had reason to believe that they were reliable sources. I still don't have any evidence that my college professors are as reliable as my teachers in high school were. And there's another problem with this argument. It proves too much. If testimony is a basic source of knowledge, then I should trust everyone. When the members of a cult tell me that the leader of their cult is an expert in all spiritual matters, then I should believe them because testimony is a basic source of knowledge. But that's crazy. I should not trust every member of every cult. So there has to be something wrong with this view.

Maya: That's a fair point. What would you say to that Steve?

Steve: The reason it isn't rational to trust religious cults is that we have evidence that they are *not* trustworthy. We have evidence *against* their being trustworthy. But that is consistent with my view. I am just saying that you should start out trusting people, and you should continue to trust them *as long as there is no evidence against their being trustworthy.* In the case of religious cults, we have evidence that the people in cults are not trustworthy, and that's why we shouldn't trust them.

Paul: But then it seems that you are trusting testimony only when there is good evidence that it is reliable. And that's just my view. So now it seems like you are agreeing with me.

Maya: No, not exactly. Steve's view is that, when it comes to trusting people, we should view them as "innocent until proven guilty." The rational position is to start out trusting people, until, or unless, you find evidence that they are *not* trustworthy. By contrast, you are saying that we need evidence for trusting them *before* we trust them, even at the very start.

Paul: Okay, I see the difference. But then I think that Steve is asking us to be really gullible. I mean, he's saying that we should start out trusting people even if we have no reason whatsoever for trusting them. That's just being gullible, isn't it?

Steve: I see what you mean, but there is no alternative to trusting people, at least initially. In a million other cases, you trust people *without* first getting evidence that they are reliable. And you have to do that, if you are to get information from them, because there is no way that you could check the reliability of everyone you listen to. It isn't feasible.

Paul: I think that all those cases of trust are based on some kind of evidence, somewhere down the line. When I was growing up, I learned whom I could trust, and whom I could not trust, by checking for myself. Eventually, I didn't have to keep checking, because I had learned from my own experience that certain people were generally trustworthy, and that people in certain situations tend to be trustworthy. But my evidence for that generalization was my own experience. For example, suppose that I stop somewhere and ask someone for directions. I had experience with certain kinds of people, and with people in certain kinds of situations, and that gave me evidence concerning whom and when to trust.

Maya: I understand what you're saying, Paul. Let's suppose you're right, at least for the sake of argument: it is rational to trust testimony only when you have good evidence that the testimony in question is likely to be true. I think that you have evidence, from your own experience, that people who claim to be experts usually *are* experts. If you think about it, you have had lots of experience with people who claim to be experts when you were growing up, and most of them really were experts.

Paul: No, I never had any experience with experts when I was growing up. Trust me. There are no experts in East Ridge, Tennessee.

Maya: But of course there are. How about your auto mechanic? Was he an expert?

Paul: I see what you mean. Yes, I suppose he was.

Maya: And how about your plumber? And your electrician? And your doctor? Were they experts?

Paul: Yes, that's true.

Maya: And they turned out to be trustworthy, right? So you have good evidence that people who are recognized as experts usually *are* experts. That gives you good reason to believe that, *in general*, people who are recognized as experts usually are experts. And that includes your professors at college.

Paul: Yeah, but there's a big difference between those experts back home and the self-appointed experts at this college.

Maya: What's that?

Paul: I first learned that my parents could be trusted, at least most of the time. Then I learned the same thing about my friends and neighbors and people at my church. Then those people told me that the local mechanic was reliable, and the same for the electrician and all the other experts in my hometown. So my trust in those experts in my hometown can be traced back to my own experience, and it is supported by that experience. But I don't have any such evidence that supports the credibility of the professors at this college. I don't know anyone who knows them. And to generalize from the case of experts at home to these experts at college is an overgeneralization. I have good reason to believe that specific people in my hometown are experts. I have no reason to believe that the professors at my college are really experts.

Steve: There *is*, actually—you can go read books and articles that will tell you that those experts have a great track record of getting things right. You could find that out.

Paul: Yes, but that will confirm the track record of the experts *only if I trust the people who wrote the books and articles that say that.* But they are just more experts, so why should I trust them?

Maya: Okay, so your view, Paul, is that it is rational to trust the testimony of someone only when that testimony is supported by evidence that can be traced back to your own experience. Is that right?

Paul: Yes. That's right.

Maya: The problem is that much of what you have learned about the world doesn't seem to fit that model.

Paul: Why not?

Maya: Just think about all the things that you read online, or in books or magazines. How often do you know anyone who knows the author of what you are reading? Not very often. But then you should not believe any of those things that you read—ever. But that can't be right, can it? Surely you have learned a lot about the world by reading, haven't you?

Paul: Well, I think that you should take everything you read with a grain of salt. You shouldn't just assume that it's true.

Maya: Here's a question for you. Do you know who Vladimir Putin is?

Paul: Of course, I'm not an idiot. He's the President of Russia.

Maya: I'm not saying that you're an idiot. Here is my point: How do you know that Vladimir Putin is the president of Russia?

Paul: Yes, I know—I read it somewhere.

Maya: That's right. And do you know any of the journalists or authors who wrote about that? Do you even know anyone who knows any of them?

Paul: No, probably not.

Maya: So if you know that Vladimir Putin is the president of Russia, it can only be because you were rational to trust the journalists and authors who told you that, even though you cannot support trusting them with evidence from your own experience.

Paul: I'm not sure about that. I might have evidence for trusting them that is complicated and hard to articulate.

Steve: Let's go back to the way you supported your trust in the experts back home. You said that you first learned that your family and friends and neighbors were trustworthy, right?

Paul: That's right.

Steve: And was it rational for you to trust them right from the beginning, without any supporting evidence that they were trustworthy?

Paul: No, I don't think so. It became rational for me to trust them after I got good evidence that they were trustworthy.

Steve: What evidence was that?

Paul: It was my own, firsthand experience. From the time I was a kid I learned that my family and friends and people in the community knew a lot of things that I didn't know. My grandmother said: "If you go fishing at Gilford Brook, you will catch poison ivy, and you will be miserable." I went to Gilford Brook anyway, and I learned that she was right. That kind of thing happened to me thousands of times.

Maya: You got poison ivy thousands of times?

Steve: I think he did, actually.

Paul: Very funny. I learned over and over again that the people in my community were generally reliable, and so I had good reason to trust them.

Steve: Fair enough. But at some point, very early on, you just trusted them, right?

Paul: Me? No!

Steve: That's right—we're talking about you here. I suppose you're right. Well, for my part, I *did* trust them, even before I knew they were reliable. And I think it was *rational* for me to do so. I didn't have to sit in a bathtub for hours, treating my poison ivy with Fels-Naptha soap, in order to learn to trust people.

Maya: Fels-Naptha soap?

Paul: It was Grandma's favorite treatment for poison ivy. Lather up with it and soak in the tub for a *very* long time. I must say, it definitely helped.

Steve: My point is that it was *rational* for you to trust people at home *right from the start*. And the same point applies to all the people who tell us that they have done research and they are experts. It is rational for us to trust them, at least to start with. And then, from there, we can learn things—we can come to *know* things that we didn't know before.

Paul: Well, I'm not sure if it was rational to trust them right from the start, but it was certainly *human*. But that's because they were my family and my community, and trusting your own family and community is just what we human beings do. But the professors here are not part of my family or my community, at least not yet, so I don't find it natural to trust them right from the start. And speaking of community, there's another point that I want to make here. You see, since it's rational for me to trust the people in my community back home, it is *not* rational for me to trust my professors in college.

Maya: Wait, what? Why is that?

Paul: I have eighteen years of experience that tell me to trust the people in my community back home. And now, my professors in college keep *contradicting* all those people back home. Since I have good reason to trust the people back home, and my professors keep contradicting the people back home, I have good reason *not* to trust my professors here. My community at home has proven trustworthy, so the very fact that my professors contradict them gives me reason to doubt my professors. And I think that applies to Steve as well. Steve has good reason to trust the people back home, as much as I do. So Steve has reason to doubt our professors too.

Steve: I think you're overstating how much our professors contradict the people back home. First of all, the people back home don't all think exactly alike. Second of all, many of the things that our professors teach are things that no one back home has ever even thought about. Sometimes that leads them to contradict things people say back home, but that's only after they have said a whole lot of things that no one back home has ever thought about.

Paul: But it often leads to a conclusion that contradicts many of the people back home.

Maya: That's a fair point, Paul.

Steve: Are you siding with him now?

Maya: No. I just think it's reasonable for Paul to consider the evidence that he has from his own experience growing up.

Paul: Thanks, Maya.

Steve: But in my view, you should trust your professors here too.

Paul: I'm not convinced of that. But suppose, for the sake of argument, that you're right. Suppose that we should start from a default position of trusting people. Then I have reason to trust the people back home, and I also have reason to trust my professors here. But sometimes those two groups of people contradict each other and when that happens, don't my reasons cancel each other out? If I were on a jury, and I heard two people give contradicting testimony, then I can't believe both of them. So what should I do?

Maya: If you have no more reason to trust one than you have to trust the other, then you should suspend judgment.

Paul: What does that mean?

Maya: It means that you do not believe either one—you don't form any opinion on the matter.

Paul: Well, I think I should continue to trust the people back home until I have reason to doubt them. But maybe I should suspend judgment about my professors, at least for the time being. I don't think I should trust them yet, but I won't distrust them either. I'll suspend judgment about them.

Maya: I don't think that goes far enough, Paul. I think that you have more reason to trust your professors than you do the people back home, at least when it comes to areas in which your professors are experts. That's because you actually have good evidence that experts figure things out before the rest of the people do, at least in the areas in which they are experts.

Paul: But we went over this already. I am not in a position to determine whether they really are experts because I cannot tell whether or not their evidence is good evidence.

Maya: But evidence is available to you that shows that your professors are part of a tradition that has a long history of discovering the truth before other people do. Throughout history, the people who study and teach at universities have discovered things before the rest of the people do, and when they make those discoveries, they often contradict the majority of the people. However, they usually turn out to be right. History is full of examples of this. Just think about all of the discoveries that have been made by experts—discoveries that are now recognized as true by everyone, including even the people in your hometown.

Paul: I think I know what you mean, but go on.

Maya: Every scientific discovery that we now accept was originally made by some expert, and at the time each discovery was made, the majority of the people would have doubted or denied that it was true. When Copernicus and Galileo first discovered that the earth revolves around the sun, most people rejected that idea as crazy. They thought: "Look, I can see that the earth is standing still. Just look at it. And I know that the sun moves, because I can watch it move across the sky with my own eyes." But they were wrong, of course, and now we all know that. And when people like Louis Pasteur first suggested that tiny, unobservable organisms caused diseases, people thought that was crazy too. History is absolutely full of examples like this. The people who study the world with scientific methods and who think very hard about things as a profession, often get things right when the majority of the people are mistaken. Your professors here are part of that long tradition. They use the same methods to study the world in the same way. That method of studying the world and thinking about things has a long history of getting things right, and you don't have to be an expert to read that history and see that for yourself.

Paul: That's a fair point, and when it comes to the natural sciences, like physics, chemistry, and biology, I would have to agree with you. But the social sciences can't use the same methods as the natural sciences, so I don't think the same argument applies to them. And even more so when it comes to the humanities—disciplines like history and philosophy are nothing like natural science.

Maya: That's true, but even those disciplines have an impressive track record of getting lots of things right before other people do.

Paul: Sometimes, yes. But at other times, they got lots of things completely wrong. I mean, both Aristotle and John Locke defended slavery. You don't think that they were right about that, do you?

Maya: No, of course not. Even great thinkers like Aristotle and Locke had biases, and sometimes those biases corrupted their thinking.

Paul: I'm glad you brought that up, because that's the other reason that I don't trust my professors here—they're all *biased*. Have you seen the statistics on how much college professors agree in their politics? They're all biased.

Steve: Are you saying that you're *not* biased?

Paul: No, not at all. If there's one thing that I have learned in college, it is that *everyone* is biased, myself included. To be honest, I really don't know *who* to trust any more, including myself, because it just seems like everyone is biased.

Maya: Well, that's a fair point. I sympathize with you on that. But I don't think you should give up on discovering the truth. Bias is a real problem, but we can overcome it.

Paul: I don't see how.

Maya: Well, I'll tell you what. I think we should continue this conversation, but I'm starving. What do you say we meet back here after dinner and continue this?

Steve: Sounds great to me. I haven't had a conversation this fun in a while.

Paul: Me too.

Maya: Okay then. I'll see you both back here after dinner. *Don't start without me!*

Chapter Two

They're All Biased!

Paul and Steve get back to the room before Maya. Contrary to Maya's request, they start talking without her.

Paul: They're all biased, Steve! They're totally biased. Everybody knows it.

Steve: Just because you disagree with someone, that doesn't make them biased. I think *you're* the one who's biased. That's why you won't listen to anyone who disagrees with you!

Paul: Oh, I listen to them all right. I don't have a choice. The mainstream media is everywhere, and they're all biased. And if I want to get a college degree, then I have to sit in class for hours listening to all these liberal professors who are even more biased.

Steve: Oh, you poor thing—having to listen to all those people who disagree with you. Maybe you need one of those safe spaces you make fun of all the time.

Paul: Well, I don't get to cancel every speaker I don't like, do I? That's what you and your friends do. It's so pathetic. Whenever someone is going to express a point of view you don't like, you just throw a big temper tantrum and make them disappear. What a bunch of babies.

Steve: I'm not going to normalize racism and sexism, Paul! And neither should you!

Paul: Oh, there it is again. Whenever anyone disagrees with you, you just call them a racist or a sexist or a Nazi. Doesn't that ever get old? It's so absurd.

Steve: I feel sorry for you, Paul. You're never going to learn anything here.

Paul: That's an ugly thing to say, Steve!

Maya returns from dinner and walks into the room, hearing their raised voices.

Maya: Hey! I told you guys not to start without me! This is what happens—you just start fighting again. I'm trying to help you. Do you want to save this friendship or not?

Steve: Sorry, Maya. This is miserable. Yes, we definitely want your help.

Paul: That's right.

Maya: Okay, let's start this over again. How did this get started?

Paul: I said that all of our professors are biased.

Maya: Okay, let's start there. Why do you think that?

Paul: Give me a minute to explain.

Maya: That's fine, go ahead.

Paul: In 2018, a professor at Brooklyn College did a study of the faculties at fifty-one of the sixty-six top-ranked colleges in the country. He looked at the political affiliations of all full-time, tenure-track faculty members with PhDs at these fifty-one colleges. It was over 18,000 faculty members. He found that the ratio of Democrats to Republicans was over 10-to-1. At almost 40 percent of these colleges, *there were no Republicans at all.* Imagine that—not a single one. In some disciplines, the ratio of Democrats to Republicans was much greater. For example, in English departments, the ratio of Democrats to Republicans was over 48-to-1. And in disciplines like anthropology and communications there were no Republicans at all. Basically, college faculties are all liberal and that makes them biased. And it also leads to lots of *group-think*—when you spend all your time with people who think just like you, then you become less open to different ideas. It just reinforces your bias. That's what happens at colleges today. Everyone just reinforces each others' biases.

Maya: College faculty these days are mostly liberal. That's true. But that doesn't prove that they are biased. You need some further argument for that.

Steve: Exactly. I think these statistics actually *support* liberal views. What you're saying is that the most well-educated, well-informed people in the country are liberals. That just goes to show that the more you learn, the more liberal you become.

Paul: The problem is that being strongly committed to a political ideology causes a person to be biased. There is good evidence for that, based on recent research. If you give me a minute, I can explain it.

Steve: Sure. Go ahead.

Paul: In 2016, some neuroscientists in California published a study of what happens in the brain when you challenge someone's deeply held political beliefs. The subjects in the study were self-identified political liberals of "deep conviction." The neuroscientists placed subjects in an fMRI scanner, to observe the activity in their brains. Then the neuroscientists showed them strong counterarguments to their political beliefs. When this was done, the subjects' brains became active in the region that is responsible for a person's sense of self. It is the part of the brain that contains your sense of who you are as a person. In other words, when these people had their political beliefs challenged, their brains responded *as if they, themselves, were under attack.* That is because they identify themselves with their political beliefs. So any attack on their political beliefs is taken as a personal attack on them.

Steve: Okay, sure. That's interesting. I'm not terribly surprised by that. Lots of people see their moral and political beliefs as part of who they are. That still doesn't show that they're biased.

Paul: Well, that's just the first part of the story. Here's the second part. Psychologists have discovered, through many years of research, that everyone suffers from what are called *self-serving biases*. When it comes to our opinion of ourselves, we are all very biased. We all think that we are much better at everything than we really are. Here is just one example to illustrate the point. Researchers gave the same questionnaire to a particular individual and to many of her closest friends and family. The questionnaire asked for an evaluation of this individual in many respects. Well, people in the study rated themselves much better, in almost every category, than their closest friends and family rated them. That's just one study out of many. There is a ton of research that supports this. Basically, we are all biased in favor of ourselves.

Steve: Okay, got it. Again, I'm not really surprised. But I still don't see what this has to do with our professors all being biased.

Paul: Well, let's put these pieces of information together, and see what follows. First, college faculties are all politically liberal. Second, people identify themselves very closely with their political beliefs. Third, we are all very biased in favor of ourselves. We do not see ourselves accurately. We overrate ourselves on a regular basis. It follows that college faculty will identify themselves with liberal political beliefs, and given their self-serving biases, they will be extremely biased in favor of liberal political beliefs. They will find evidence to support those beliefs, and they will deny or disregard any evidence to the contrary of those beliefs.

Steve: Okay. I have a *bunch* of objections to that argument.

Paul: Of course you do. I bet I know exactly which part of your brain is active right now.

Steve: Very funny. But you won't get off that easy. My first objection is that you are being inconsistent. Look at your evidence. It all comes from *experts*—experts in psychology and neuroscience. And most of those people are professors at colleges and universities, just like this one. You say that we should not trust college professors, so why are you appealing to all of their research as evidence?

Paul: I see your point, but in this case, I think they just confirmed something that we all knew already, from our own experience. I already knew that people with deep convictions see those convictions as part of who they are, and I also knew that this makes them biased. I learned all of that from my own experience. I just used the research in psychology to convince you because I know that you trust all that stuff. For me, it's all just common sense.

Maya: You know, there is a way for Paul to appeal to this research, even though he himself doesn't trust it.

Steve: How is that?

Maya: You and I trust the experts, including our professors here. Paul can argue that since *we* trust the experts, and the experts' own research implies that they are biased, it follows that we should *not* trust them after all. In other words, if we do trust them, then given what their research tells us, it follows that we should *not* trust them. It might sound odd, but that happens sometimes.

Steve: Whoa. Hold on. You lost me there. Can you explain that again?

Maya: I learned about this is my logic class. There is a type of argument called a *reductio ad absurdum*. That's just Latin for "reduction to absurdity." Here is how it works. You assume something, for the sake of argument, and then you show that this assumption leads to a contradiction. Since the assumption leads to a contradiction, the assumption cannot be true. Here is an example. Suppose that I believe that I should trust Tom. Then Tom tells me, very sincerely, that he is a chronic liar. I also believe that I should *not* trust chronic liars. Now, these three beliefs, taken together, lead to a contradiction. If I believe that I should trust Tom, and Tom says that he is a chronic liar, then I should believe that Tom is a chronic liar. But I also believe that I should not trust chronic liars, and since I now believe that Tom is a chronic liar, it follows that I should *not* trust Tom. So my beliefs imply that I *should* trust Tom and that I *should not* trust Tom. That is a contradiction. It follows that one of my original beliefs must be false.

Steve: Okay, I think I get that. But how is that relevant to Paul appealing to the experts even when he says he doesn't?

Maya: Well, Paul can argue like this. Let's assume, for the sake of argument, that we should trust our professors. Our professors are politically liberal, and their own research shows that political beliefs will make a person biased with respect to anything related to politics. It follows that our professors will be biased with respect to anything related to politics. We should not trust people who are biased. Therefore we should not trust our professors, at least when it comes to anything related to politics. So if we assume that we *should* trust our professors, then it follows that we really *should not* trust our professors. The assumption that we should trust them entails both that we should trust them and that we should not trust them. That's a contradiction. So our original assumption—that we should trust our professors—cannot be true. Paul can argue in this way even if he, himself, never trusts our professors. The point of the argument is that anyone who *does* trust college professors will be led to a contradiction and that shows that they should stop trusting them.

Paul: Wow. Did I hear somewhere that you are planning to go to law school?

Maya: Yes, that's right.

Paul: Well, if I ever need a lawyer, I will look you up. That was amazing.

Maya: Well, that's very nice of you to say. Thank you. But now I have to tell you—I think that there's a really big problem with your argument.

Paul: Okay. I'm listening.

Maya: Everything you said about political belief and bias is true. You're right about all of that. But you left out something very important. The evidence indicates clearly that those facts apply to *everyone*. Everyone who has strong political convictions identifies with those convictions. And everyone is biased when it comes to their very identity. So everyone is going to be biased when it comes to closely held political beliefs. That is what the evidence tells us. Everyone is biased, *and that includes you*. You are not somehow magically immune to bias.

Paul: Even if you're right, I don't think that affects my argument here. Suppose that everyone is biased. "Everyone" includes our professors, so our professors are biased. That's my point, and I don't think you've contradicted it. You've just pointed out that even more people are biased, but that doesn't change the fact that our professors are biased, and that's all I need for my argument. Since they are biased, we shouldn't trust them.

Maya: But you haven't thought this through all the way. You are arguing that since our professors are biased, we should not trust them. That argument assumes that, in general, if someone is biased, then you should not trust them. But the evidence tells us that everyone is biased, in the same ways. So if we should not trust people who are biased, then we should not trust anyone at all. In fact, if you reason in this way—discrediting everyone who is biased, then to be consistent, you have to discredit yourself and stop trusting yourself. That's the only way for you to be consistent. But you aren't discrediting yourself, are you? You continue to trust yourself, right? Well, if you trust yourself, even though you know you are biased, then in order to be consistent you cannot discredit other people simply because they are biased.

Paul: I see your point. But, to be honest, I *don't* think that I'm biased— at least not as biased as our professors are. I know that might sound implausible, but hear me out. Each one of us can look into our own minds and tell what we are thinking. I can look into my own mind and I can check to see if I am biased. Sometimes I *am* biased, and I can tell that. But when it comes to issues of morality and politics, I have checked and I know that I am *not* biased. I realize that this amounts to claiming that I am exceptional, but I can tell by examining my own mind, and I'm telling you that I am not biased—at least not nearly as biased as our professors are. Maybe it's because I have less invested in being right or something. I don't know. But I can honestly tell you that on most of these issues, I am not biased.

Steve: Paul—*everyone* thinks that! Everyone thinks that they are not biased. But the evidence tells us that they are usually mistaken. Why should you be any different?

Paul: I know what you mean, but look—I can look inside my own mind and see what I am thinking, and that's how I can tell that I am not biased. But I can't look inside other people's minds and see what they are thinking, so I have to rely on the evidence about most people, which says that they are biased. I think that's the only rational approach to take. When it comes to myself, I have to look into my own mind and examine myself, to see if I am biased, but when it comes to other people, all that I can do is to rely on the evidence about their brains and their behavior. When I do those things, I am led to the conclusion that they are biased and I am not. I know that might sound arrogant, but where did my reasoning go wrong? I can't see where it did.

Maya: I understand what you mean, but that is exactly how it seems to everyone. Here's a fun fact: studies have found that *everyone thinks that they are less biased than everyone else.* That's right—*everyone* thinks that. That isn't because it's true, of course, since it couldn't be true. It is not possible for everyone to be less biased than everyone else. The reason everyone thinks this is that we have what psychologists call a *bias blind spot.* Simply put, our biases are hidden from us; they are not readily available to the conscious mind. When you look within yourself, you can see the parts of your mind that are available to consciousness, but there is a lot more of your mind that you *cannot* see, and that includes a whole lot of your biases. So when people look within themselves, they don't see any bias, so they infer that they are not biased. But when they observe the behavior of other people, they can see from their behavior that other people are very biased. Thus, people infer that other people are biased, but they, themselves, are not. But the truth is that they are just as biased as everyone else. It's just that they cannot detect their own biases by looking within themselves, so they don't know that they are there. Thus, we get the bias blind spot.

Paul: But why should I think that any of that applies to me? I mean, I was never a subject in any of those studies. Maybe I'm an exception to the rule.

Maya: It's certainly *possible* that you are an exception to the rule, but it's extremely improbable, especially if you start to look at your own behavior.

Paul: What do you mean?

Maya: First, remember all the facts about our self-serving biases. We are always biased in favor of ourselves. We paint ourselves in a very flattering light, even when the truth is much less flattering. Study after study has found that this is true of everyone—we all have self-serving biases. Now, if you were under the influence of your self-serving bias, what would you say to yourself about your own biases? If you were being self-serving, would you say: "I am just as biased as everyone else?" Or would you tell yourself: "I am much less biased than everyone else"?

Paul: It would be more self-serving to think that I am less biased than everyone else.

Maya: That's right. So think about this. We know that almost everyone who has been studied has a self-serving bias. And we know that almost everyone who has been studied thinks that they are less biased than everyone else. Of course, this is exactly what we would expect from someone who is under the influence of a self-serving bias. And now we know that you also say that you are less biased than everyone else. And, as with everyone else, if you are under the influence of a self-serving bias, then that is exactly what you would say—that you are less biased than everyone else. In light of those facts, which is more probable, that your self-serving bias leads you to think that you are less biased, even though it's false, or that you alone are really and truly less biased than everyone else?

Paul: Okay, okay. I get the point. I suppose it's much more likely that I am just as biased as everyone else. Now, remind me again why I can't just accept this and keep the rest of my view.

Maya: Think of it this way. There is a dilemma here. Either the fact that someone is biased discredits them completely, or it does *not* discredit them completely. If bias discredits a person completely, then since everyone is biased, everyone is completely discredited, including you. In that case, you can discredit your professors only if you are also willing to discredit absolutely everyone, including yourself. This would be a kind of skepticism, in which you think that no one can be trusted, at least when it comes to things like politics. So you stop trusting anyone, including even yourself. You could do that, but that's what you would have to do, in order to be consistent. So suppose that you take the other horn of the dilemma—bias does *not* discredit a person completely. Then the fact that our professors are biased does not discredit them completely, and you cannot dismiss their opinions just because they are biased.

Paul: Okay, that seems fair. But when I know that someone is biased, surely that gives me reason to discredit them *at least a little bit*, doesn't it?

Maya: Well, here's the problem. Remember that our biases are hidden from us, and they are often acting on us. When you discredit the opinion of someone else because you think they are biased, how do you know that this isn't just *your own biases* finding a way to defend your own beliefs? You see, that's the problem. Attributing bias to other people is often just an effect of our own, self-serving biases. So when you discredit another person by attributing bias to them, it is possible, and maybe even likely, that you are just exercising your own biases.

Paul: Hmm. Yes, I see your point.

Steve: The more I think about this, the more disturbing I find it.

Maya: What do you mean?

Steve: Well, in my psychology class we learned about a whole bunch of cognitive biases. The list is a mile long. And as I recall, the evidence shows that we are all subject to these biases. When you add them all up, it starts to look like everyone is biased all the time. But if that's true, then I really wonder if we should trust anyone, including even ourselves, when it comes to anything that really matters.

Paul: That seems crazy. You can't really think that.

Steve: I'm just worried about it. To really get the point, I think you need to know just how extensive these biases are.

Paul: Okay, go ahead.

Steve: Let's start with *confirmation bias*. We all look for evidence that supports our beliefs. When we hear something that supports our beliefs, we accept it uncritically. But when we are given evidence that contradicts our beliefs, then we scrutinize it very carefully, and find some way to reject it. Everyone is like this. In one experiment, people were presented with two studies on whether the death penalty deters crime. One study found that the death penalty did deter crime, while the other study found that it did not. The two studies used different methods. One study compared the crime rates before and after the implementation of the death penalty in particular states. The other study compared the crime rate in states that had the death penalty with the crime rate in states that did not have the death penalty. The subjects in the experiment read both studies. Then they were asked which of these two methods was more reliable. The subjects picked whichever method was used in the study that supported their prior opinion about the death penalty. They chose to believe whatever would confirm their prior beliefs. There are a whole bunch of other studies that have found the very same thing. We look for evidence that confirms our preconceptions, and we ignore any evidence that contradicts them.

Paul: I'm not really surprised by that.

Steve: You can see the effects of this in the real world, too. Every year, many people are wrongfully convicted of crimes that they did not commit. In 2018 alone, over 150 people were wrongfully convicted. Criminologists who have studied these wrongful convictions have found that the main cause of wrongful convictions is actually confirmation bias. Once investigators form an opinion about who committed the crime, they look for evidence that confirms their opinion, and they ignore any evidence that contradicts their opinion. The result is that many innocent people are prosecuted and convicted.

Maya: Wow. That's terrible.

Steve: Then there is the *anchoring bias*. The first piece of information that you receive about something becomes your "anchor." It will influence your subsequent thinking in ways that are irrational. For example, if you see a designer T-shirt for $40, and then you see another designer T-shirt for $30, then you will think that the second T-shirt is a good deal. But if you first see a designer T-shirt for $10, and then you see one for $30, then you will think that the second one is way too expensive. The only difference between the two cases is in what you saw before you saw the $30 T-shirt. Your belief about the price of the $30 shirt is shaped by what you saw first, but that is completely irrelevant to whether the $30 T-shirt is a good deal or not. There are tons of examples of this.

Paul: Thirty dollars for a T-shirt is crazy.

Steve: Then there is the *availability bias*. If we can easily think of an example of something, then we tend to believe that it is more common than it really is. For example, people hear about homicides all the time. But they hear about suicides much less often. So most people believe that there are more homicides than suicides. But that's actually false. There are more suicides than homicides. And then there is the *framing bias*. You can state the very same fact in two different ways, and people will react very differently to the two statements, even though they state the very same fact. For example, if you tell someone that a certain operation fails 80 percent of the time, then they are likely to see it as a bad choice. But if you tell them that the operation succeeds 20 percent of the time, then they are more likely to see it as a worthy option. Of course, this is the very same fact that is being stated in two different ways, but those two ways of framing it lead people to see it differently. That's completely irrational. And then there is the *group-think* that Paul mentioned back before dinner. That is a real bias too. In one experiment, researchers asked people if it was permissible to suspend free speech when society felt threatened. When people were alone, only 19 percent answered "yes." But when they were put in a group of four other people, all of whom said yes, then the percentage of people who agreed jumped to 58 percent.

Paul: Yup, I knew it.

Steve: And there are many more of these biases. We often think we see patterns where they do not really exist. We think that we have more control over things than we really have. We tend to blame people for misfortunes that are not their fault. These are just a few of the many cognitive biases that psychologists have discovered. When you see the whole list of them, it's kind of shocking.

Maya: So what do you make of all that? What are you implying?

Steve: Well, if I'm honest with myself, then I know that I am subject to all of the same cognitive biases that everyone else is—the self-serving bias, the confirmation bias, the anchoring bias, the availability bias, and all the others. Those biases cause us to think in ways that are unreliable. They lead us to believe things that are false. Since I am subject to all of these biases, and they lead us to believe things that are false, then it seems that most of my beliefs are probably false, because they have all been produced by biases. Of course, the same argument applies to everyone. So, in light of all these biases, I am starting to think that I really shouldn't trust anyone on much of anything, including myself.

Paul: I have three words for you: *No. More. Mushrooms.*

Steve: Yeah, yeah. Very funny.

Paul: Isn't this just another good reason to doubt all this research? Remember the ongoing replication crisis in psychology? A whole lot of experiments in psychology cannot be replicated. They do them again, and they don't get the same results. I think you should take all that research on cognitive biases a lot less seriously. How do we know that it will be replicated? Maybe it was all bad research.

Steve: I see your point, but the amount of research that demonstrates these biases is really large. Study after study has found the very same biases in everyone. I find it really hard to believe that none of that research was onto something.

Paul: But the conclusion that you are led to is crazy. How can you stop trusting yourself and everyone else about everything? That's impossible.

Steve: Well, this reasoning doesn't apply to everything. I can still trust my own eyes and ears most of the time, and I can trust other people in areas where biases aren't really involved. If I ask you if the gas station on the corner is still open, then you are not likely to be biased about that. So I don't have to doubt everyone about everything. It's just when it comes to areas where people are biased that I have these doubts. When it comes to those areas, I wonder if I should really stop believing very much. Maybe I should just say, "I don't know," and leave it at that.

Maya: Let me see if I understand your argument, Steve. It goes like this. We are all subject to cognitive biases. Those biases distort our thinking, which makes it unreliable. Therefore our thinking is unreliable. When our thinking is unreliable, we make mistakes and form false beliefs. Now that we know all of this about ourselves, we should stop holding beliefs in any areas in which we might be biased. Is that the argument?

Steve: Yes, that's right. I'm not saying that I actually I believe that. I'm just starting to wonder about it. Every step in the argument seems right to me, so I don't see how to avoid that conclusion.

Maya: I understand that. If recent psychology is right, then human beings aren't as rational as we once thought we were. That's true. But I don't think you have to stop trusting yourself and everyone else. We need to distinguish three different conclusions that you might draw from these facts.

(1) *Sometime*s our biases make us *completely unreliable*.
(2) Our biases *always* make us *less reliable* than we would be without them.
(3) Our biases *always* make us *completely unreliable*.

The first statement says that it is sometimes true that our cognitive biases completely destroy our ability to get the right answer. That is what happens in some of the experiments that you cited. So I think it's fair to say that the research supports (1)—sometimes we are completely unreliable. But notice that is just *sometimes*. It isn't all the time. Of course, our cognitive biases are always there, in some sense, and it is reasonable to infer that they always make us *less reliable* than we would be if we were not biased. That is what (2) says—we are always *less reliable* than if we were unbiased. But notice—being less reliable is not the same thing as being *completely unreliable.* The conclusion that you are inferring from the research is what I called (3)—that our biases *always* make us *completely unreliable.* But I don't think that the existence of cognitive biases shows that we are always completely unreliable.

Steve: Why not?

Maya: Well, our cognitive biases are not our only mental characteristics. We also have a lot of cognitive skills, and when we exercise those skills we can figure things out, despite our biases. So at least on some occasions, our cognitive skills might get us to the right answer, despite our cognitive biases.

Steve: That's certainly possible. But I think that even the first of the three conclusions should lead us to doubt ourselves. The first conclusion says that sometimes our cognitive biases make us completely unreliable. That is what seems to happen in many of the experiments and real life stories I mentioned. People's cognitive biases make them think in ways that are completely unreliable. So that does happen—sometimes our biases make us think in ways that are completely unreliable. Now, remember that we cannot tell when we are under the influence of our cognitive biases. Our cognitive biases are not transparent to us. So at any given time, I might be under the influence of a cognitive bias and I would not know it, because I cannot tell when that is happening. Of course, I will always *seem* to be unbiased to myself, but that is just because my biases are hidden from me. So I can never really know if my current thinking is trustworthy, or if it is just the product of my own biases. That's the situation I am in all the time. I cannot tell if my current thinking is just the product of cognitive bias. And if it *is* biased, then it is also possible that the bias is making me completely unreliable. Since I can never really tell whether this is happening, I should really doubt myself all the time, at least when that is possible.

Paul: I think you just graduated from mushrooms to something stronger. But I see your point.

Maya: I think there is a good response to your argument, but in order to explain it, I will have to take a detour through another argument from the history of philosophy. Is that okay?

Steve: Yeah, sure.

Maya: In my very first philosophy class, I learned about a famous argument from the French philosopher René Descartes. It goes like this. It is possible for you to have a dream in which everything seems exactly the way it seems right now. In your dream, you are sitting in your dorm room, having a conversation with Paul and me. You see the things in your room and you hear the sound of my voice. But it's all part of a dream. You are dreaming it. That's possible, right?

Steve: Yeah, sure, I suppose so. My dreams are usually a little weirder than that.

Maya: Yes, that's true for most of us, but it is possible that you have a dream in which this happens, right?

Steve: Yes, that seems possible.

Maya: Well, if you were having a dream like that, you would not know that you were dreaming. You would think that everything happening in the dream was real, because it would seem real—it would seem just like this. So you would have no way of knowing that you were really dreaming, rather than awake. So here is a question: How do you know that you are not dreaming right now? How do you know that this is not just a dream?

Steve: Well, I remember waking up this morning and getting out of bed and having breakfast. And I did not lie down to take a nap at any time after that.

Maya: Could all of those things happen in a dream? Could you have a dream in which you wake up, get out of bed, have breakfast, and stay awake after that? Could you dream all that?

Steve: Well, sure, I guess so.

Maya: Then seeming to wake up and get out of bed and have breakfast does not prove that you are not dreaming right now, since all of those things could happen in a dream. If you were dreaming right now, you would say to yourself: "I know I'm not dreaming, because I remember getting out of bed this morning." But that would just be part of the dream. So the fact that you seem to remember getting out of bed does not prove that you are not dreaming right now.

Paul: Okay, but I could pinch myself right now, to see if I am awake. Actually, I will pinch Steve instead.

Steve: Ouch! Cut it out!

Paul: Steve, I'm helping you here. I just proved that you are not dreaming.

Steve: Remind me to thank you later.

Maya: But Paul, you know what I'm going to ask you. Could all of that happen in a dream? Could you have a dream, in which you pinch Steve, to prove that he is awake? Isn't that possible?

Paul: Yes, I suppose it is.

Maya: Here's the point: there is no experience that you could have that would prove that you are not dreaming, because for any experience whatsoever, you could have that experience in a dream. So no matter what you experience—seeming to get out of bed, pinching yourself, and so on—that experience could just be part of your dream. No matter what you experience, it is always still possible that you are just dreaming. So there is no way to prove that you are not dreaming.

Paul: So this is what LSD is like. Mushrooms were just the gateway drug for you people.

Steve: Okay, I see your point, but what does any of this have to do with my argument about bias?

Maya: The main point of your argument was that you could not tell, at any given time, if your thinking was just caused by your bias. It is always possible, that at any time, you are under the influence of bias, and since your biases are hidden from you, you cannot tell if you are under the influence of bias. And if you *are* under the influence of bias, then your thinking is unreliable and your beliefs are probably false. So the possibility of being under the influence of bias is a good reason to doubt your own judgment all the time. That was your argument, right?

Steve: Yes, that's right.

Maya: Well, in just the same way, it is always possible that you are dreaming, and if you were dreaming, then you would not be able to tell that you were dreaming. And if you were dreaming, then your beliefs would be false. Just as it is possible that your present thinking is biased, so it is possible that you are dreaming right now. If the mere possibility that you are under the influence of bias is a good reason to doubt your own judgment, then by the same reasoning, the mere possibility that you are dreaming is a good enough reason to doubt that you are awake right now.

Paul: Peyote anyone? Ayahuasca perhaps?

Steve: I don't see how those arguments are the same. My argument is based on the fact that we are biased, which we know is true. Your argument is based on the possibility that we are dreaming, which we have no reason to believe is true.

Maya: But remember—what we know, from the research, is that we have biases that influence us sometimes. We do *not* know that they are *always* influencing us in ways that make us *completely unreliable*. That is possible, but we do not have sufficient evidence to believe that. What we have reason to believe is that it is possible, at any given time, we are under the influence of a cognitive bias that makes us completely unreliable. That is a possibility. Your argument is that just that possibility—a possibility of error—is a good enough reason to doubt your own judgment. In the same way, the Dream Argument (as I'll call it) argues that just the possibility that we are dreaming—which is also a possibility of error—is a good enough reason to doubt that we are awake. In both cases, the mere possibility of error is given as a reason to doubt our own judgment.

Steve: Okay, yes, I see what you mean. So you think that I should even doubt that I am awake right now?

Maya: No, I do not think that. Here is what I think. I think that both your argument from bias and the Dream Argument make the same mistake. The mistake is to think that the mere possibility of error is a good reason to doubt your own judgment. I think that is false. The mere possibility that you are mistaken is not a sufficient reason to doubt your own judgment, even if it is impossible to rule out that possibility. In the case of dreaming, I think that is clear to common sense. It is possible that we are dreaming right now, and there is no way for us to prove that we are not. But it does not follow from that possibility alone that we should doubt we are awake. We are justified in trusting our own senses until we have some positive reason to think that we are mistaken. The mere possibility of error should not cause us to doubt ourselves. And the same goes for the possibility that our cognitive biases make us completely unreliable thinkers. The mere possibility that we are that biased is not a sufficient reason to doubt our own judgment.

Paul: I think the acid trip is over.

Steve: But it seems to me that there is a difference between the possibility that I am dreaming right now and the possibility that I am under the influence of bias right now. The possibility that I am dreaming right now is very *remote*. In order for me to be dreaming right now, the world would have to be very, very different from the way I believe it to be. In the actual world, I don't have dreams that are this vivid, complete in every detail, or last this long. So in order for me to be dreaming right now, the world would have to contain dreams that are completely unlike any that I've ever had. Now, I realize that is *possible*, but it seems like a very remote possibility. By contrast, the possibility that I am under the influence of bias does not seem remote at all. In the world as it is, I know that everyone has cognitive biases, and that these biases influence our thinking very often. So the possibility that I am under the influence of bias seems like a much more relevant possibility—one that I should take more seriously than the possibility that I am dreaming.

Maya: Yes, I see your point.

Paul: Wait a minute, I have a question about this. Doesn't this argument defeat itself?

Steve: What do you mean?

Paul: Well, what you are saying is that whenever you think about a subject in which you might be biased, you cannot trust your own thinking. But that very subject—the subject of bias and how it affects you—is a subject in which you might be biased, right? So if you are consistent, then you should apply this concern about bias *to itself*. But then you would stop trusting this reason for doubting yourself. Do you see what I mean?

Steve: I'm not sure.

Maya: Paul is saying that the position that you are considering is self-defeating. That means that the position itself logically entails that you should not accept it.

Steve: Okay, you lost me there.

Maya: Your argument for doubting yourself whenever you might be biased is an instance of reasoning—you are reasoning to that conclusion. But if you doubt your own reasoning whenever you might be biased, then that very reasoning seems like just the sort of thing that you should doubt. So if you doubt yourself whenever you might be biased, then you should doubt the very reasoning that led you to that conclusion. And at the end, you have no trustworthy reason to doubt yourself.

Steve: Okay, I think I get that. But I'm not sure that my position is really self-defeating in that way.

Maya: Why not?

Steve: Well, most of the evidence tells us that we are biased in favor of ourselves, and we seek to confirm our previously held opinions. If I were under the influence of those biases, then I would not come to the conclusion that I cannot trust myself. That's not the sort of belief that a self-serving bias or a confirmation bias would lead me to. So I think I have good reason to think that this particular argument is *not* the product of bias.

Paul: Okay, I see your point.

Maya: Look, I agree that you should take the possibility of bias seriously. But I still don't think that it should lead you to stop trusting yourself completely whenever you might be biased.

Steve: Okay. Why not?

Maya: Let's start with this. As rational beings, we have two goals: we want to believe what is true, and we want to avoid believing what is false. We want to acquire knowledge and we want to avoid error.

Steve: That seems right.

Maya: Now notice something. These two goals actually pull us in opposite directions.

Steve: What do you mean?

Maya: Suppose that your only goal was to believe everything that is true. Then what would you believe?

Paul: Everything. You would believe everything.

Maya: That's right. By believing everything, you would believe every truth—or at least every truth you can grasp.

Steve: But you would also believe a bunch of falsehoods too.

Maya: That's right. That's why no one would decide to believe absolutely everything, because we also want to avoid error. Now suppose that your only goal was to avoid believing anything false. Then what would you believe?

Steve: Nothing. You would believe nothing at all.

Maya: That's right. By believing nothing at all, you would avoid believing anything false.

Paul: But then you would miss out on knowing lots of truths.

Maya: That's right. When you think about it, you can see that these two goals—believing truth and avoiding error—actually pull us in opposite directions. As truth seekers, we want to believe, in order to know the truth, but as error avoiders, we want to withhold our belief, so as to avoid error. Our goal of believing what is true gives us a reason to trust both others and ourselves, while our goal of avoiding error gives us a reason to be cautious and withhold judgment.

Steve: That seems right.

Maya: Some people prioritize believing what is true, and err on the side of credulity, while other people prioritize avoiding error, and err on the side of suspicion and doubt. But everyone has both goals, at least to some extent. And now here is my point. If you want to know the truth, then you have to trust yourself, at least to some extent. You have to trust that you have the ability to find the truth. That means that you have to trust yourself to overcome your own biases, at least well enough to discover the truth.

Steve: But how do I know that I can do that? How do I know that I can overcome my own biases?

Maya: Maybe you *don't* know that. But the only way to attain knowledge, if there is any knowledge to be had, is to take a chance. It's risky; that's true. But if there is knowledge out there to be had, then I think the risk is worth it. So I think that you should treat yourself as innocent until proven guilty, for the sake of pursuing knowledge, in case there is knowledge to be found.

Steve: Does that mean that I can just ignore all of my cognitive biases? Just pretend that I am completely unbiased?

Maya: No, I wouldn't say that. That would not be a good way to pursue the truth.

Steve: Then what am I supposed to do about my biases? I don't think I can get rid of them.

Maya: No, you can't really get rid of them. But you can counteract them.

Steve: How so?

Maya: From what I have read, there are strategies that you can use to counteract your biases. First of all, for any opinion that you hold, consider the alternatives to your opinion. What are the other possibilities? Identify those alternatives. Then ask yourself: "How do I know that my opinion is right, rather than one of these alternatives?" Identify your reasons for holding your opinion. What is your evidence for your opinion? Then, finally, ask yourself if that is really good evidence for your view. And at this point, you should force yourself to follow good rules of reasoning. Don't give yourself any slack.

Paul: What would be an example of that?

Maya: Well, suppose that you believe a conspiracy theory because you read it on the internet. You have only read one source on the subject, and you believed that source.

Paul: What's wrong with that? I thought it was okay to trust testimony because it is innocent until proven guilty.

Maya: Yes, I think that's true, but sometimes we have evidence that a source is often guilty. When we know that a source is often mistaken, then we should *not* continue to trust that source without independent evidence. A case in point is the internet—we know that the internet is full of misinformation. So that source is definitely guilty, unless it is used with caution.

Paul: Well, it can't be any worse than the mainstream media. If you ask me, the internet is a much *better* source of information than all the mainstream media.

Steve groans audibly.

Maya: What is it?

Steve: Paul believes all sorts of conspiracy theories that he finds on the internet.

Paul: I'm not saying they're *all* true. But I certainly think that some of them are. You're just too narrow-minded to even consider them.

Steve: Please. Don't get me started.

Maya: You know, it's getting late. What do you say we pick this up tomorrow morning, after breakfast? I don't have any classes in the morning.

Paul: Neither do I.

Steve: Neither do I.

Maya: Then let's start again in the morning. What do you say?

Steve: Sounds good to me.

Paul: Me too.

Maya: Okay, good. I'll see you both in the morning.

Chapter Three

I Read It on the Internet

Late the next morning, the group meets again, as planned. Steve starts the conversation.

Steve: If you ask me, one of the biggest problems with our society today is that people go to the internet for all of their information. They get on the internet, and they believe everything they read. But the internet is full of conspiracy theories and misinformation. So people end up with all sorts of crazy, false beliefs. That's often why you and I disagree, Paul. You get on the internet and read some crazy conspiracy theory, and then I have to spend the next several weeks trying to talk you out of it. The internet has been bad in lots of ways, because it has led to the spread of so much misinformation. I wish you would stop getting all of your news online.

Paul: I disagree. The internet has made people more informed than ever before. It has made knowledge available to everyone. Things that used to be hidden from the majority of the people are now revealed to everyone, and that's a good thing. Here's just one recent example. In 2010 and 2011, WikiLeaks.org published a set of classified videos and documents related to the wars in Iraq and Afghanistan. The world was shocked. The videos and documents showed horrible things happening in Iraq and Afghanistan that no one knew about. The mainstream press didn't discover it; WikiLeaks did. And now the people—*all* the people—know things that their government was trying to hide. That's the power of the internet. In order to have a true democracy, the people need to know what's really happening in the world. The internet does that for them. The internet has democratized information. Through the internet, knowledge belongs to the people—*all* the people, not just a few elites who want to control what everyone thinks.

Steve: I disagree. It's true that the internet has sometimes given people information like that, but it's also completely full of *mis*information—lies and propaganda. And the problem is that the average person cannot tell the difference between the accurate information and the misinformation. So the average person is just as likely to believe the lies as to find the truth.

Paul: But if the goal is to gain knowledge, surely it is better to have more information out there, available to everyone. How could it be worse to have more accurate information available? How could you be opposed to the dissemination of more knowledge?

Steve: Consider this example. The Argentinian author Jorge Luis Borges once wrote a story, "The Library of Babel," about a library that contains an almost infinite number of books. The books are about every subject—physics, chemistry, biology, psychology, history, politics, law, and so on. Everything you could ever want to know is contained in a book somewhere in this library. But the library also includes just as many books that are full of nonsense and lies. Now imagine that you are trapped in this library. You might think that you could learn anything you want to know in the library. But there is a problem. Since you are trapped in the library, with no access to anything outside of it, you have no way of knowing which books contain accurate information and which books contain nonsense and lies. There is no way for you to tell, just by looking at the books, which are which. And that's the problem with the internet. It's full of accurate information, but it's also full of *misinformation*. So when you go on the internet, you are just as likely to find falsehoods as you are to find truths.

Paul: But if you happen to find accurate information, like I always do, then you will have true beliefs, like I do.

Steve: Your modesty is overwhelming. But even if you *do* happen to form a true belief, it will just be by accident. It will be because you were *lucky*. Getting a true belief by accident might be fine in the short run, but in the long run your luck will run out, and you will wind up believing lots of stuff that is completely false.

Maya: And if a belief is true just by accident, then it isn't really *knowledge*. You might happen to have a true belief, but you won't really *know* that it's true.

Paul: Why not?

Maya: I'm actually learning about this in class right now. Here is an example to illustrate the point. Suppose that I buy a lottery ticket, and I really want to believe that it is the winning ticket. I want to believe it so badly that I actually manage to convince myself that it's true—this really is the winning ticket. I have no reason to believe it. I have no evidence that this is the winning lottery ticket. But I believe it anyway, just out of wishful thinking. Now suppose that it just so happens that this *is* the winning ticket. Then my belief is true. But did I *know* that this was the winning ticket?

Paul: No, you didn't. You just made a lucky guess.

Maya: That's right. I was just lucky. My belief was true, but it's only by accident that it's true, and that isn't knowledge. Knowledge is true belief that isn't true just by accident.

Paul: So if I happen to stumble onto some accurate information on the internet, and I believe it, then I might have a true belief, but I wouldn't really know that it was true.

Maya: That's right. Think of it this way. You stumbled onto some accurate information, but you could just as well have stumbled onto some misinformation, and then you would have believed something false.

Paul: So what more is required for knowledge?

Maya: There's a lot of debate about that. Here is one way to think about knowledge that will work for our purposes. Knowledge is true belief that is produced by *intellectual virtues*, not by *intellectual vices*.

Paul: That sounds awfully moralistic.

Maya: Yes, I know. But when you understand how these terms are used, you'll see that it really isn't. An intellectual virtue is a mental habit—it's a way of thinking—that is reliable. When I say that it's reliable, I mean that it leads to more true beliefs than false beliefs. For example, having the habit of listening to both sides in a dispute, rather than just listening to one side, is an intellectual virtue. Someone who has the habit of listening to both sides in a dispute will get to the truth much more often than someone who just listens to one side. It will lead to more true beliefs and fewer false beliefs over time. By contrast, the habit of just listening to one side in a dispute would be an intellectual vice, because it will lead to more false beliefs than true beliefs over time. Intellectual virtues are ways of thinking that are generally reliable—they lead to more true beliefs than false beliefs. By contrast, intellectual vices are generally unreliable—they lead to more false beliefs than true beliefs.

Paul: Okay, I get that. What does that have to do with knowledge?

Maya: Well, remember that knowledge is a true belief that is not just true by accident. When you have knowledge, it isn't just an accident that your belief is true. Well, what would make it *not* an accident that your belief is true? If your belief were formed by one or more intellectual virtues—habits that tend to lead to true beliefs—then it would not be an accident that your belief is true. Intellectual virtues are reliable ways of thinking. So if a belief was produced by an intellectual virtue, then it is likely to be true. And then, if it *is* true, it will not be an accident that it is true. That's knowledge.

Steve: I'm still processing this. Could you illustrate it with an example?

Maya: Sure. Think of Sherlock Holmes. He is very observant. That is an intellectual virtue, because being observant will lead to more true beliefs than false ones. He also asks a lot of questions. That's also an intellectual virtue, because it will lead to finding out more relevant information. He also thinks critically—he doesn't just believe everything people tell him. That's an intellectual virtue too, because it helps him to avoid error. Sherlock Holmes has a long list of intellectual virtues—habits of mind that lead to more true beliefs than false beliefs. Consequently, when Holmes investigates a crime, and he exercises his intellectual virtues, it is no accident that he figures out the truth about who committed the crime. His intellectual virtues produce mostly true beliefs, so it is no accident when they lead him to the truth. When Holmes's beliefs are produced by his intellectual virtues, and his beliefs are true, then he *knows*. That's the idea. Knowledge is true belief that is produced by intellectual virtues—habits of mind that are generally reliable.

Steve: Okay, well, in that case, people don't get knowledge just by going to the internet. The habit of just looking things up on the internet and believing whatever you read is not an intellectual virtue. That habit leads to as many false beliefs as true ones.

Paul: If people just surfed the internet blindly, without ever using their own judgment, then that would be true. But almost no one surfs the internet blindly, believing whatever they read. People use their own judgment to determine what to believe. Those people have intellectual virtues, and when they exercise those virtues, they acquire knowledge. So I still think most people get knowledge from the internet.

Steve: But the average person doesn't have intellectual virtues, Paul. I mean, where would they get them? Two-thirds of Americans do not have a college degree, and almost 40 percent of them never attend college at all—not for a single day. Where would they get any intellectual virtues? What they have are mostly intellectual vices. That's why they believe all sorts of crazy things they read on the internet.

Paul: Ahh . . . *There* it is.

Maya: There's what?

Paul: Your elitism. Your classism.

Steve: Oh, please. Not this again.

Maya: Hold on, Steve. What do you mean, Paul?

Paul: Educated people think they're the only ones who know anything, and everyone else is an idiot. It's elitism. It's classism. They think they have all the answers all the time. That's why they think they should be in charge of everything. And that's why they hate the internet. Before the internet, the elites could control the flow of information. They did this by controlling which opinions counted as knowledge. Only doctors had medical knowledge. Only lawyers had legal knowledge. Only government officials and pundits had knowledge of public affairs. The elites could control what counted as knowledge. If it wasn't in the *New York Times* or the *Wall Street Journal*, or some other establishment publication, then it was just rumor, or hearsay, or conspiracy theory. Then along came the internet and changed all that. All of a sudden, *everyone* had a platform. And the elites hated it. They could no longer control what people see and hear and think. They could no longer control what counts as knowledge. So now they're trying to turn the clock back. That's why they want Facebook to decide what is true and false. God forbid that the rabble should do it for themselves. But it's too late. The internet has given knowledge back to the people. Since knowledge is power, that gives power back to the people. And that's what democracy is all about. Power to the people.

Steve: Are we supposed to sing something now? Are you announcing your campaign today?

Paul: Maybe I should.

Steve: I find that frightening.

Maya: Let's talk about this. Believe it or not, I don't completely disagree with you, Paul. In some ways, the internet has been a real force for democracy. The Arab Spring would not have happened without the internet, and that was definitely a movement for democracy. Whenever the internet gives knowledge and power back to the people, then I support that. I am all for it. But the issue is how often the internet really achieves that, and I have my doubts about that.

Paul: Why do you doubt it?

Maya: I don't think uneducated people are idiots. They know lots of things that highly educated people don't know. But I don't think the internet is bringing out the best in people. On the contrary, I think it often brings out the worst in us. When it comes to our thinking, it activates many of our worst biases and prejudices. It encourages our intellectual vices.

Paul: How so?

Maya: When I first explained the ideas of intellectual virtue and intellectual vice, I used the example of listening to both sides in a dispute. Remember that?

Paul: Yes. The habit of listening to both sides in a dispute is an intellectual virtue, and the habit of listening to just one side is an intellectual vice.

Maya: And we agree on that, right?

Paul: Yes, absolutely.

Maya: Well, when people get on the internet, most of them go straight to sources that agree with them. They read sources that support their preconceived opinion, whatever it is, and they ignore sources that contradict their view. They do not seek out alternative points of view. So they live in what my professor calls an *epistemic bubble*.

Paul: That sounds like a personal problem.

Maya: Very funny, but it isn't just a personal problem. To be in an epistemic bubble is to be isolated from sources of information that might contradict your opinions. If you are in an epistemic bubble, then you only get information from sources that agree with you.

Paul: Why is that so bad?

Maya: If you only get information from sources that agree with you, then if there is evidence out there that shows that you are mistaken, you will not hear it, because it is outside your epistemic bubble. So if you are mistaken about something, you won't be able to figure that out.

Paul: Okay, I see your point. Of course, if your opinion is true, then that's okay though, isn't it?

Maya: You could have a true belief, but you wouldn't know that it was true.

Paul: Why not?

Maya: It's another case of just getting lucky.

Paul: How so?

Maya: If you live in an epistemic bubble, then whenever you have a false belief, you will not discover that, because you are ignoring any evidence that would show you are mistaken. So even on those occasions when your belief is true, you were really just lucky that ignoring all the evidence to the contrary didn't matter that time. So you might have a true belief, but just by luck.

Paul: And a lucky true belief isn't knowledge.

Maya: Right.

Steve: I've also heard people talk about *echo chambers*. Is that the same thing as an epistemic bubble?

Maya: An echo chamber is actually worse than an epistemic bubble. In an epistemic bubble, people do not hear all the evidence, but if they *did* hear it, then they would listen to it. By contrast, in an echo chamber, people reject any evidence that comes from outside sources that do not share their opinion.

Paul: And that's worse?

Maya: Yes, I think it is. If you're in an epistemic bubble, then you might not get all the relevant evidence, but *if* you heard that evidence, then you would listen to it and perhaps even change your mind. In an echo chamber, not only do you lack relevant evidence, but also you would reject it even if you heard it.

Steve: Yes, I see your point. Someone in an epistemic bubble might not hear all the relevant evidence, but if she did hear it, then she would be willing to listen to it and perhaps correct her mistake. By contrast, someone in an echo chamber would simply dismiss that evidence altogether.

Paul: I see the difference between an epistemic bubble and an echo chamber, but I'm not convinced that an echo chamber is really much worse than an epistemic bubble.

Steve: Why not?

Paul: Well, if people remain within their epistemic bubbles, then they will never hear any evidence that contradicts their opinions. In that case, the fact that they *would* listen to the evidence *if* they heard it is irrelevant, since they will never hear it. So if people remain in their epistemic bubbles, then those bubbles might as well be echo chambers.

Maya: True. But there is still this difference between the two. For people in an epistemic bubble, you can correct their mistakes just by exposing them to the evidence that they were not getting. But if they're in an echo chamber, then even if you show them the evidence they were missing, that will not lead them to correct their mistake. So it is more difficult to correct the mistakes of people who are in echo chambers than the mistakes of people who are in epistemic bubbles.

Paul: I suppose that's true. But what if one of these echo chambers just happens to be right? What if one of them has all true beliefs? Let's call this the Correct Echo Chamber. If you happen to be in the Correct Echo Chamber, then ignoring evidence to the contrary is actually a more reliable way of forming beliefs, right?

Maya: But how do you know that your echo chamber is the correct echo chamber? Think about how many different echo chambers are out there—all with different sets of beliefs. The many different echo chambers in the world all say different things—they all contradict each other. So most of them have to be wrong about some things. What are the chances that, out of all those many different echo chambers, yours just happens to be the correct echo chamber?

Paul: Yes, I see your point.

Maya: And even if you did just happen to belong to the One Correct Echo Chamber, you would just have been lucky to happen to be in that one. So, again, your beliefs might be true, but you wouldn't really have knowledge.

Paul: But maybe that's the best we can do. Maybe being lucky to be in the right group is as good as it gets.

Maya: But it *isn't* the best we can do. There is an old saying that "two heads are better than one." Well, it turns out that there is empirical evidence for this. Recent work in psychology has found that groups of people, working together, outperform individuals working alone on a wide range of intellectual tasks. Groups of people, working together, are actually better at finding the right answer to a question than individuals working alone. In fact, studies have shown that a group of people working together will outperform even the smartest individuals working alone. The reason is that, in a group, a person who finds the right answer is often able to persuade the others, with good reasons and arguments, that it is the right answer.

Steve: Were the other people just intimidated by this person's confidence?

Maya: No. The researchers were interested in that question, so they designed the experiment to determine if that was the case. They found that good arguments for the correct answer persuaded people more often than confidence. It was actually the good reasoning that persuaded people in the group.

Steve: Wow, that's really encouraging.

Maya: Yes, it is. What the experiment showed is that two heads really are better than one. When people reason together, in collaboration, and listen to each other, then they are more likely to get the right answer than if they just think alone. So collaborative thinking is more reliable than thinking alone.

Paul: But that isn't happening on the internet, is it?

Maya: No, it isn't. Collaborative thinking requires that you listen to the opinions of people who disagree with you. That way, if you are mistaken, you have a chance to figure that out. Otherwise, if you are mistaken, you will never figure that out, because you are only listening to people who hold the same mistaken opinion as you. Since we are all fallible, we should give ourselves the chance to figure out if we are mistaken. The best way to do that is to listen to people who don't agree with you. But the internet is taking us away from that. It's encouraging us to ignore anyone we disagree with.

Paul: Fair enough, I see your point. Certainly when it comes to anything controversial, that sounds right. The internet isn't making us more thoughtful about controversial things. But at least when it comes to basic facts, you can always get those on the internet. I know there is misinformation out there, but if you're careful, and you check multiple sources, then you can at least get the basic facts. That was my point when we first started this conversation.

Organizations like WikiLeaks have revealed facts that people never would have known if it were not for the internet. So when it comes to basic facts, I still think we're better off with the internet than we were without it.

Maya: Sometimes that's true. But even when you learn some facts on the internet, you don't necessarily *understand* them.

Paul: What do you mean?

Maya: Understanding a fact involves more than just knowing it. Understanding a fact involves knowing how it is related to other facts. To understand a fact, you have to see how it fits into a larger pattern of facts. For example, suppose you go online and you read that wages for most Americans have stagnated since the 1970s. That's true. It's a fact. But even when you know that fact, you don't automatically understand it. In order to understand it, you need to understand how it fits in with other facts about the American economy over the last fifty years. You would also need to understand some economics. If you understood those things, then you might understand why this fact about wages in America is a fact. But that's what it would take to understand this fact, and you can't get that understanding just by finding isolated facts on the internet. In order to gain understanding, you need knowledge of some general patterns in the world. That's what a good *theory* does for us—it gives us knowledge of general patterns, which we can then use to make sense of particular facts.

Paul: Yeah, sure, I agree with all that. You need good theories to explain how all the facts fit together. Absolutely. But you can learn good theories on the internet too. I have learned lots of good theories on the internet.

Steve: But how can you tell which theories on the internet are good theories, and which theories are bad theories? We're right back in "The Library of Babel" again, aren't we?

Paul: Well, what's the alternative? It's *gatekeepers*. You want all of our information filtered through a select group of people who decide which theories we should accept. But that method has a serious problem.

Steve: What's that?

Paul: If you have a reliable set of gatekeepers—people who generally get it right, then the people will get reliable information, including reliable theories. But if you have an *unreliable* set of gatekeepers—people who tend to get it wrong, then the people will get unreliable information and bad theories. So I would say that if you get your information from good gatekeepers, you were just lucky, because they could just as well have been bad gatekeepers, so you wouldn't really get knowledge that way either.

Steve: Now you sound like you're becoming skeptical of every source.

Paul: No, I'm not. I just think that we need a real competition of ideas in the public square. Maya is right—we are more reliable when we think together, in collaboration. But if the gatekeepers of information all think alike, then they will not give us competing ideas, and then we will just be following one set of prejudices—those of the gatekeepers. So I think we need multiple, independent sources of information. We need independent media. But that's what you find on the internet. So I still think we're better off with the internet than without it.

Maya: But then what about the problem of people listening to just one side, and ignoring everything else?

Paul: I agree that we need to teach people to listen to different points of view with an open mind, as much and as often as possible. If people will acquire that habit—that intellectual virtue—then I think the internet will be a reliable source of knowledge.

Steve: Well, I can accept that for some points of view, but I'm not listening to any crazy conspiracy theories. That's just beyond the pale for me. There need to be some limits here.

Paul: Ahh, yes, "conspiracy theories."

Steve: Oh Lord, here we go.

Paul: That term has been *weaponized*. By calling something a "conspiracy theory," you automatically exclude it from rational consideration without having to give any reasons or evidence at all. It's a term of abuse that is meant to shut people down before they start. And those people, who get shut down, just happen to be people who are questioning those in authority. What a coincidence. It's name-calling, pure and simple, and that should make any rational person suspicious of it.

Steve: Sometimes the label is accurate, Paul.

Paul: But then why would you need to use it? People use a term of abuse when they want to shut down a conversation before it starts. And why would someone want to do that?

Steve: I'm guessing you're about to tell us.

Paul: They shut it down because the evidence on their side isn't nearly as good as they pretend it is.

Steve: Not necessarily. Sometimes people just get impatient with theories that are too crazy to take seriously.

Paul: I'm sure that's how you feel, but that attitude isn't as justified as you think it is.

Steve: You're a smart person, Paul. I can't believe you would take conspiracy theories seriously. They're completely insane. I mean, there are people out there who believe that intelligent reptiles, disguised as humans, are living among us and plotting to destroy us. Are you telling me I should take that idea seriously?

Paul: No, of course not. That's crazy. But there are other conspiracy theories that are not so crazy, and I think some of those theories should be taken more seriously than they are.

Maya: Well, maybe we should define the term "conspiracy theory," so we all agree on what we're talking about.

Steve: I agree. Here's a try. A conspiracy is when a group of people act together, in secret, to achieve some goal. And a theory is an explanation of something. If we put those two definitions together, we could say that a conspiracy theory is a theory that explains some event in terms of a group of people acting together in secret to achieve some goal.

Paul: That sounds right.

Maya: Well, that's a good start, but I think there's still something missing from that definition. Osama bin Laden and his associates acted together, in secret, to attack and destroy the World Trade Center.

Paul: So they say, so they say.

Maya: My point is that their actions constituted a conspiracy—a group of people acting together, in secret, to achieve a goal. So our definition implies that the theory that they destroyed the World Trade Center is a conspiracy theory, because it explains that event in terms of a conspiracy. But that's not right. That explanation is not a conspiracy theory.

Paul: That's right. A conspiracy theory is always a theory that is offered as an *alternative* to the official story. A theory counts as a conspiracy theory only if there is some official account, usually given by people in authority, and the conspiracy theory is a *rival* account. That seems to be necessary for any theory to count as a conspiracy theory.

Steve: Yes, I agree. That's right. Conspiracy theorists are always doubting or denying the official story. Now that I think about it, they are people who don't trust the people in authority, and that's why they are inclined to doubt what they say, and accept a conspiracy theory instead. So it comes down to trust. That keeps coming up in our conversations. So many things come down to trust.

Paul: Yeah, I agree. I wouldn't have realized that, but it's true.

Steve: So tell me, Paul, why are conspiracy theorists so suspicious of people in positions of authority? It seems a bit paranoid, doesn't it?

Paul: No, I don't think it is. Look, we know that conspiracies happen, especially when people in power are involved. People in the Nixon administration conspired to steal the 1972 election. That's a fact. We know that. People in the Reagan administration conspired to sell arms to Iran, illegally, and then channel that money to the Contras in Central America. The Bush-Cheney administration conspired to mislead Congress and the American people about the evidence for weapons of mass destruction in Iraq. These are just a few examples. We know that conspiracies happen.

Steve: Yes, but in all these cases the conspiracies were uncovered, so everyone now knows that these things happened. So these explanations aren't really conspiracy theories.

Paul: My point is that we all know that conspiracies happen. There is no doubt about that. So the only difference between you and the conspiracy theorist is that the conspiracy theorist believes that there have also been *undetected* conspiracies. Now, why is that irrational?

Steve: I think that your own description answers that question. To say that they are "undetected" conspiracies is precisely to say that there is no evidence for them. But if there is no evidence for them, then there is no reason to believe them, and if there is no reason to believe them, then it is irrational to believe them.

Paul: Well, I think that there is *some* evidence for these theories. It's just not *conclusive* evidence. The evidence is just not sufficient to prove that these theories are true.

Steve: But if they haven't been proven, then we shouldn't believe them, should we?

Paul: Look, if a conspiracy succeeds, then the conspirators will not be discovered. In that case, there will be no proof of a conspiracy, precisely because the conspiracy succeeded. So if anyone has ever gotten away with a conspiracy, then we do not have any proof of that, just because they got away with it. So if you refuse to believe any conspiracy theory without proof, then you are assuming that *no one has ever gotten away with a conspiracy.* But why would you believe that? Why would you believe that no one has ever gotten away with a conspiracy?

Steve: I don't deny that anyone has ever gotten away with a conspiracy. I'm just demanding convincing evidence before I will accept any *particular* conspiracy theory. There's a difference here. But I want to come back to the fact that conspiracy theories are always given as alternatives to an official account of what happened. The official account usually gives a good explanation of what happened, and that's why I think it's irrational to accept a conspiracy theory. If there were no good explanation of some event, then it might be rational to consider a conspiracy theory. But as we've agreed, all conspiracy theories are given as alternatives to an official, widely accepted account. In that case, it seems to make more sense to accept the official account, rather than believe a conspiracy theory.

Paul: The official explanations in these cases always leave some facts unexplained. That's why conspiracy theorists don't buy those accounts. On 9/11, firefighters and other eyewitnesses said that they heard explosions after the planes had hit the World Trade Center. Why would they be hearing more explosions? And there was evidence of extremely high temperatures at the World Trade Center—molten metal, hot wind, and scorched cars. Why would people hear additional explosions after the planes had struck? Why would the collapse of the towers cause extremely high temperatures? The official account of the destruction of the

World Trade Center does not explain those facts. That is why conspiracy theorists reject the official account of what happened.

Steve: There are actually good explanations of those facts. If you listen to a scientist explain what happened, they could explain those facts. But suppose that the official account does leave some facts unexplained. That doesn't show that the official account is false. The correct explanation of an event will often leave some details unexplained. For example, suppose that we have good evidence that a fire was caused by an arsonist who set the fire with gasoline and a match. We might not know why he chose to start the fire in one room rather than another, but that, by itself, should not cast any doubt on the explanation. Even a good explanation might leave some details unexplained. To demand that a good explanation explain every single detail is to demand too much. So even if the official explanation of the destruction of the World Trade Center on 9/11 leaves some facts unexplained, that is not a good reason to reject that explanation.

Paul: But the more a theory can explain, the better. That's generally accepted in science and everyday life. If my theory can explain facts that your theory cannot explain, then at least in that respect, my theory is a better theory than your theory.

Steve: Sure, but there are usually facts that the official story actually explains better than the conspiracy theories do. In addition, conspiracy theories have to make lots of assumptions that we have no independent reason to believe. They have to assume that many government officials are lying about what really happened, and that no one has been able to detect those lies. That is certainly possible, but the more a theory has to assume, the less plausible it becomes, at least when compared to theories that assume less.

Paul: Okay. So the official explanation assumes less. That's true. But the conspiracy theory sometimes explains more of the facts.

That's one point to the official explanation, and one point to the conspiracy theory. That sounds like a tie to me. It certainly doesn't show that conspiracy theories are irrational.

Steve: Well, I don't think we can score it quite that simply, but I see your point. To be honest, I think that conspiracy theorists are irrational because they are *paranoid*, and paranoia is an intellectual vice.

Paul: This might just get us somewhere. Go on. I'm listening.

Steve: I'm going to use the idea of intellectual vices to make the point. As Maya put it, an intellectual vice is a way of thinking that leads to more false beliefs than true beliefs. Well, it seems to me that paranoia is an intellectual vice. A paranoid person is someone who has a habit of thinking that people are out to get them—conspiring against them. And it's usually false. So paranoia is an intellectual vice—it's a way of thinking that leads to more false beliefs than true ones. I think conspiracy theorists are paranoid. They have a habit of thinking that people are conspiring against them and that habit is generally unreliable. It leads to more false beliefs than true beliefs. They might be right once in a while, but they're usually wrong. Since conspiracy theorists are paranoid, and we should not be paranoid, we shouldn't be conspiracy theorists. That's my argument.

Paul: Now I think we're getting to the heart of the matter. Let me start with this. In December 2019, the *Washington Post* won the release of 2,000 pages of government documents that revealed that government officials had been lying to the American public about the war in Afghanistan for eighteen years. The documents contained interviews with more than 400 people who played a direct role in the war in Afghanistan—generals, diplomats, aid workers, and Afghan officials. It took the *Washington Post* over three years to win the release of these documents. The documents show that everyone was lying about the war in Afghanistan, in every way. The war was never "winnable." Nothing we did in

Afghanistan was working—nothing at all. But everyone in the military and in the government said that it was. They were all lying, *and for eighteen years!* The cost of all those lies, both in terms of money and human life, is staggering. Roughly 157,000 people died in that war. Think about that. And it is estimated that we spent somewhere between $930 billion and $980 billion on the war, and that's not even counting whatever the CIA spent. So we probably spent over one trillion dollars on a war that was a complete disaster, from start to finish. And the evidence for that claim—that it was a complete disaster—comes right from the people who were on the ground, in the middle of it—over 400 of them.

Steve: Okay, I get it. What's your point?

Paul: People in power *lie*. And they don't just lie a little bit. They lie *a lot*. I mean they lied about that war constantly for eighteen years. And that isn't even the first time that has happened. Ever hear of the *Pentagon Papers*? They were the government documents that were released in the early 1970s that revealed that the government had been lying for years about the war in Vietnam. The story about the war in Afghanistan is just "same song, second verse . . ." But it isn't even the second verse. It's like the ten-thousandth verse. So here is my reply to your claim that conspiracy theorists are paranoid. I would say that those who trust people in power to such a degree that they refuse to consider conspiracy theories are *naïve*. And if paranoia is an intellectual vice, then so is *naïveté*.

Maya: I think Paul has a point here.

Paul: Paranoid people trust other people *too little*. That's true. But naïve people trust other people *too much*. I would say that these are both intellectual vices. If you are paranoid, then you will form a lot of false beliefs about people conspiring against you. But if you are naïve, then you will form a lot of false beliefs about the government telling you the truth when it isn't. People who uncritically believe conspiracy theories are paranoid. That's true. But people who refuse to consider the possibility that some conspiracy theories are true are naïve, and I think that's just as bad.

Steve: Yeah, I guess I can agree with that. But what does that mean for conspiracy theories?

Maya: That's a good question. What would you say, Paul? Throughout this conversation, you have avoided defending any particular conspiracy theory. I was a bit surprised by that. I kept expecting you to pick one and defend it, but you never did. Do you really believe any conspiracy theories, or were you just playing devil's advocate?

Paul: Well, I believe that the moon landing was staged and filmed in Arizona, but that's not really a conspiracy theory, since it's an established fact, right?

Steve: Very funny. I don't think even *you* believe that one. Seriously, which ones do you believe?

Paul: Well, I'm not going to say it *out loud*. You never know who might be listening.

Steve: You're impossible. Look, I see where you're coming from, but I just can't accept any conspiracy theories. They all still seem paranoid to me.

Maya: Okay, so you both agree that paranoia is an intellectual vice, and you also agree that naiveté is an intellectual vice. But you still disagree about conspiracy theories. Steve thinks that conspiracy theorists are paranoid, while Paul thinks that those who reject all conspiracy theories are being naïve.

Paul: That's right. So what do you think, Maya?

Maya: Well, it occurs to me that the answer actually depends on which situation we're in.

Steve: What do you mean?

Maya: Well, if the people in authority in our society are generally trustworthy, then entertaining conspiracy theories is paranoid, as Steve thinks. But if the people in authority in our society are often lying to us, then rejecting conspiracy theories is naïve, as Paul thinks. So the answer depends on which situation we're actually in.

Paul: So which is it? What do you think?

Maya: I agree that both paranoia and naiveté are intellectual vices, and I think that the appropriate attitude is somewhere in between the two. There is an intellectual virtue in between these two vices—the virtue of trusting people in authority enough, without trusting them too much. This actually fits a pattern that was first noticed by the ancient Greek philosopher Aristotle. Aristotle noticed that many virtues are "in between" two vices. For example, courage is the virtue of responding in the right way to danger, and that includes feeling the appropriate amount of fear. Someone who feels too much fear is cowardly, and someone who feels too little fear is foolhardy. The courageous person is sort of "in between" the coward and the fool. Where the coward feels too much fear, and the fool feels too little fear, the courageous person feels just the right amount of fear and acts accordingly. Well, courage is a moral virtue, not an intellectual virtue, but it sounds like the same point applies here. The paranoid person trusts people too little, and the naïve person trusts people too much. Those are both vices. Somewhere in between those vices, there must be a virtue of trusting people just the right amount.

Steve: Okay, that makes sense. But then how would this intellectual virtue treat conspiracy theories?

Maya: You don't have to believe any specific conspiracy theory in order to be genuinely open to the possibility that some of them are true. You might not even have an opinion about which ones are true. You might just be open to the possibility that some of them are true. And you might even qualify that opinion a bit more. A conspiracy theory could be partially true or somewhat "close to the truth" even if it isn't entirely, exactly right. So here is a position that one might take toward conspiracy theories. You might say: "I take seriously the possibility that some of the conspiracy theories that are out there are at least partially true or somewhat close to the truth. I don't know which ones, but there's a decent chance that some of them are partially true. Therefore, I read them enough to take them seriously, even if I don't actually accept any one of them fully." That's the view I would take.

Steve: Hmm, that's interesting. I'm a bit surprised that you would consider them at all, but I admit that I'll have to think about it some more.

Maya: That's fair enough.

Paul: In the meantime, I guess that you and I still disagree completely, Steve.

Steve: Yeah, that's right. No surprise there, I guess. But I think I do understand your position a bit better than I did before.

Paul: Same here.

Maya: You know, I wonder if the very fact that the two of you still disagree should lead each of you to doubt your own opinion.

Steve: What do you mean?

Maya: Well, I have known both of you for several months now, and the two of you seem equally intelligent, equally thoughtful, equally well informed, and about equally biased. So as far as I can tell, the two of you are about equally likely to be right about an issue like this.

Paul: Obviously you really don't know us very well, or you would have seen my complete and utter superiority to Steve by now.

Steve: Especially when it comes to modesty.

Paul: But seriously, why should that lead me to doubt my own opinion?

Maya: Well, think of it this way. If you recognize that Steve is just as intelligent as you are, just as thoughtful as you are, just as well informed as you are, and no more biased than you are, then why would you think that you are any more likely to get to the truth than he is? Objectively speaking, you should recognize that he is just as likely to be right as you are. But then, if he is just as likely to be right as you are, and he disagrees with you about this, then it is just as likely that he is right and that you are wrong as the other way around.

Steve: Hmm, I don't like where this is going, because the very same argument applies to me, doesn't it?

Maya: Yup, that's right.

Paul: Well, I want to continue this conversation, but I'm starving. What do you say we meet back here after lunch and class and continue this?

Steve: That works for me.

Maya: That sounds good. I'll see you guys this afternoon.

Chapter Four

We Still Disagree

After lunch, Maya returns to the room to find Paul and Steve waiting for her. Before she even sits down, Steve launches right in.

Steve: I don't understand, Maya. You seem to be saying that whenever two people disagree, they should both give up their beliefs. That's insane!

Paul: Completely! If everyone did that, the world would be full of spineless cowards!

Maya: Well, well. Look at you two—shoulder-to-shoulder, agreeing with each other. That's a nice change. But you didn't describe my view accurately. Could you calm down and let me explain the argument?

Steve: Yes, of course.

Maya: To explain the argument, I need to start by defining a technical term. Suppose that two people are equally likely to know the truth about something. Given their background knowledge, their intelligence, and their level of bias, they are equally reliable in this area. Then philosophers say that these two people are *epistemic peers.*

Steve: Can you give me an example?

Maya: Sure. Suppose that you two do equally well at basic arithmetic. Now suppose that I give you both a simple math problem. Suppose that you both take the same amount of time to work on the problem, and you are equally careful and attentive in working on it. Then you would both be equally likely to get the right answer. We would say that the two of you are epistemic peers with respect to the answer to the math problem.

Steve: Okay, I get that.

Maya: Now let's put that example into a specific context. Suppose that the two of you go out to dinner with a group of friends and at the end of dinner, you need to split the check. Each of you gets a copy of the check and each of you calculates how much each person owes. But when you have done your calculations, you get two different results—you come to two different conclusions about what each person owes. Now suppose that Paul says: "My answer is right. There's no doubt about it. Steve must have made a mistake. So everyone pay the amount that I told you to pay." Paul doesn't double-check, or ask Steve how he got his answer, or anything like that. He just believes, very confidently, that his answer is right, and Steve's answer is wrong. Now what would you think about that?

Steve: That's Paul. What did you expect?

Paul: Very funny.

Steve: Seriously, though—it would be dogmatic and irrational for Paul to think that he was right and I was wrong. We are both equally good at math, and we were equally careful in calculating. He is just as likely to have made a mistake as I am. So why should he think that I made a mistake, rather than that he made a mistake? He shouldn't believe that.

Maya: That's right.

Paul: Wait a minute. Is it obviously irrational to believe that?

Maya: Well, consider an analogy. Suppose that you have two thermometers in your house, and they have both worked reliably for years. One day, the two thermometers give two different readings. What should you infer?

Paul: One of them is wrong.

Maya: Yes. But, which one?

Paul: There's no way to know—at least not without using some other device.

Maya: That's right. Since both thermometers have been equally reliable in the past, you have no way to tell which one is accurate and which one is inaccurate now. If you just picked one of the two thermometers and said, "I think this one is right, and the other one is wrong," that would be irrational, wouldn't it?

Paul: Yes, I suppose so.

Maya: Well, when it comes to calculating the check at dinner, you and Steve are just like those two thermometers. Up until now, you have both been equally reliable when it comes to simple math. So there is no reason to prefer one of your answers to the other one. To pick your own answer and say, "This one is right," is just as arbitrary and irrational as picking one of the two thermometers and saying, "This one is right, and the other one is wrong." So once you know that Steve got a different result, you should suspend judgment about whether your answer is correct.

Paul: Okay, I see your point about the dinner check. But that is an unusual case. Most cases of disagreement are very different from that.

Steve: How so?

Paul: In the case of the dinner check, it's easy for two people to be epistemic peers. As long as they have the same basic math ability and they are equally attentive, they will be epistemic peers with respect to the answer. That is because the issue is just an issue of simple math. But most issues are not like that. Most issues are way more complicated than that.

Steve: Yeah, but why does that matter?

Paul: Consider a person's belief about something like climate change. What facts about a person are relevant to their reliability with respect to climate change?

Steve: Well, background knowledge, I suppose.

Paul: Yes, and that's not all. How intelligent are they? How much time have they spent thinking about this issue? How attentive have they been when they thought about it? How biased are they on this issue? Are they generally open-minded or closed-minded? Have they been distracted when they thought about it? And on and on. My point is that there are *many factors* that will influence a person's beliefs about something like climate change, and all those factors are relevant to the person's reliability in the area of climate change. So in order for two people to be epistemic peers with respect to climate change, they would have to be exactly alike in every single one of these respects. Now, how likely is it that any two people are exactly alike in every one of these respects? Not very likely. So in most cases, no two people will ever be epistemic peers.

Maya: Yes, that's true. But I don't think that really solves the problem of disagreement.

Paul: Why not?

Maya: In many cases, you cannot tell whether it is you or the other person who is epistemically superior. And that is precisely because there are so many relevant factors, and they all influence a person's reliability on an issue. There are lots of differences between you and Steve—in all of the ways that you just mentioned. You have different background knowledge, different kinds of intelligence, different biases, and so on. Now, how do you know that your traits make you more reliable than Steve on any given issue? In this case, and many others like it, I think it is impossible for you to know that. And again, that is precisely because the relevant factors are so complicated. Even if one person has more background knowledge, that person might be so biased that it cancels out the value of their background knowledge. Even if one person is more intelligent, they might have spent less time or been less attentive to the issue in question. So in many cases, it is impossible to tell which person in a disagreement is more reliable.

Paul: Okay, sure. But if they're not actually epistemic peers, then your argument still doesn't work. Your argument was that people who are epistemic peers have to suspend judgment in a disagreement. But you now agree that people in a disagreement are almost never epistemic peers. So your argument doesn't work, does it?

Maya: I think I can restate the argument, based on the fact that you cannot tell who is more reliable in a disagreement. Here's the new argument. It often happens that someone disagrees with you, and as far as you can tell, this person could be your epistemic peer or even your epistemic superior. In that situation, you should suspend judgment about who is right and who is wrong. For all you know, this person is more reliable than you are on this issue, so you have no reason to prefer your own belief to theirs. So you should suspend judgment about whether your original belief is true.

Steve: Hmm.

Paul: I just can't believe that's right.

Steve: Neither do I.

Maya: The view that I am defending is called the *Equal Weight View*— in a disagreement between two people, in which you can't tell that one is superior to the other, you should give equal weight to both views. That means that you should suspend judgment about which one is right and which one is wrong. Here is another argument for the view: Suppose that you are on a jury and you hear two experts testify about something. One testifies for the prosecution and the other testifies for the defense. They both seem well qualified. If one of them is more reliable than the other, you cannot tell which one it is. Now, how should you weigh these two testimonies?

Steve: You should give them equal weight.

Maya: That's right. Now, if you should give equal weight to the beliefs of two other people in that situation, then to be consistent, shouldn't you do the same thing when one of the two people involved in the disagreement is you? In the expert testimony case, you have agreed that if you cannot tell who is more reliable, then you should give each testimony equal weight. Well, if you are one of the two people involved, but the situation is otherwise the same, then shouldn't you do the same thing? It seems to me that you should. If you disagree with another person, and you have no good reason to think that you are generally more reliable in this area than the other person, then you should treat yourself and the other person in the same way you would treat the testimony of the two experts. You should give both opinions equal weight. Since you disagree, that means that you should suspend judgment.

Paul: But in a lot of cases, I think I *can* tell who is epistemically superior in a disagreement.

Steve: And let me guess—it's you.

Paul: Yeah, so what? What's wrong with that?

Steve: Remember all those self-serving biases we talked about? We are all extremely biased in our own favor. We *all* think that we know better than everyone else. So *of course* each of us thinks that we are more reliable than the person we disagree with. But that's just because we are biased in favor of ourselves. If we are honest and objective, we often disagree with people who are just as smart and thoughtful and well informed as we are, at least as far as we can tell. In those situations, we don't really know that we are more reliable than they are.

Paul: So you agree with Maya now? You and I both have to suspend judgment about everything we disagree on?

Steve: Oh, hell no.

Paul: Thank you! But then what's wrong with her argument?

Maya: That is the question, isn't it?

Steve: Look, it seems to me that there really *is* a relevant difference between me and everyone else.

Paul: I think that's what I said, and it didn't work.

Steve: That's not what I mean. Hear me out. There are some things that are essentially *private*. Some experiences, including what I would call *insights*, are things that one person cannot fully communicate to another person. You can describe it to another person, but you cannot make them have the same experience or insight.

Paul: I need an example.

Steve: Let's start with an experience. Suppose that you are red-green color blind. There is nothing I can do to enable you to know what the color red looks like. I can describe it to you, but that is not the same thing as having the experience of seeing the color red. So no matter what I tell you, to try to describe it to you, I cannot give you the same experience as I have.

Paul: Okay, sure.

Steve: Well, I think some insights are like that. Here's an example. There are some people who can calculate the sum of two large numbers instantaneously. Give them two large numbers and they can just *see*, mentally, the correct sum. That's an unusual example, but I think that we all have our own insights sometimes. You just see that something is true. When you have an insight like this, you can certainly tell other people that you have had this insight, but you cannot *give it to them*—you cannot make them have the same insight, at least not with words.

Paul: Now that you mention it, there are other examples of information that you cannot communicate to another person. As Steve knows, when I was growing up, my family was poor. At the end of every month, we did not know how we were going to pay the next month's rent and have enough money left to buy groceries.

So at the end of every month, my brothers and sisters and I went all around the house to find anything that we might be able to sell. We took it down to the flea market on Dodds Avenue and got what we could for it. After years of doing that, there was nothing left in the house to sell. My father worked whatever odd jobs he could find, but it was never enough. One night at midnight, working third shift, he dropped dead of a heart attack. He was fifty-two years old. Sometimes I tell people that story, to try to get them to understand what it's like to be poor. But they never really get it—at least not as far as I can tell. If they didn't grow up poor, then there's nothing I could tell them to convey *what it feels like* to grow up poor. So that would be something that you just can't communicate to another person.

Steve: Yeah, I know what you mean. And I think that provides a possible response to Maya's argument. If you have an experience or an insight that you cannot fully communicate to another person, then I think you have good reason to believe that you are in a better position to know the truth about something than they are. And that means that you have good reason to trust your own opinion, even if it seems like they know just as much as you do.

Maya: We sometimes know things that are impossible to communicate to another person. That's true. But I don't think that will solve the disagreement problem. First, everyone is capable of having these incommunicable experiences and insights. So when you have a disagreement with another person and you have incommunicable experiences or insights, remember that, for all you know, the other person also has incommunicable experiences or insights. And those experiences or insights might put them in an even better position to know the truth about the issue in question. Second, your experiences or insights might improve your ability to know the truth about something, but they can still lead you to a mistaken conclusion.

Paul: How so?

Maya: Imagine two people who are arguing about whether or not we should legalize drugs like cocaine and heroin. One of them is a recovering addict, and he knows what it's like to be addicted to drugs. For that reason, he is of the opinion that these drugs should remain illegal. And he thinks that he is in a better position to know the truth about this, because he has had experiences that the other person has not had, and he cannot communicate these experiences fully to the other person. So he tells himself: "I know that he disagrees with me, but that is because he doesn't know what I know, which is what it's like to be addicted to drugs." But the other person in the dispute knows some things that he doesn't know. He knows exactly how much violent crime and mass incarceration are caused by the fact that these drugs are illegal and the drug trade is so lucrative. He knows that if you legalized these drugs, all that violent crime and mass incarceration would cease.

Paul: I'm not sure that I agree with that.

Maya: I'm just using this as a hypothetical example to illustrate something. I'm not trying to settle the debate over legalization here. Just treat this as a hypothetical example.

Paul: Okay, that's fine.

Maya: Well, in this situation, one person has an incommunicable experience that is definitely relevant to the issue. They know what it's like to be an addict and just how painful that is; so they do know something that the other person doesn't know. But the other person has more background knowledge that is relevant. They know that decriminalizing drug possession in other countries has not led to significant increases in the use of drugs or in the rate of addiction to drugs. In this situation, the person who has more background knowledge might be in a better position to know the truth about this than the person who has the incommunicable experience.

Paul: Yes, I suppose so.

Maya: So even if you have an incommunicable experience or insight, the person who disagrees with you might still be in a better position to know the truth than you.

Steve: Okay, fair enough. But my own opinions still *seem* true to me, and surely that should count for something. When I think things over, and I take into account that other people disagree with me, the opinions that I hold still seem true to me. You're telling me to disregard that, but that can't be right.

Maya: I'm not telling you to disregard that. I'm telling you to weigh that together with all the other evidence you have, including the fact that *everyone else's opinion seems true to them.* Some of those people disagree with you, and as far as you can tell, they are in at least as good a position as you to get the right answer.

Paul: It now occurs to me that your argument is based on a questionable assumption.

Maya: What's that?

Paul: You say that the fact that Steve disagrees with me is a reason for me to doubt my own opinion. That assumes that the mere fact that Steve believes something is somehow evidence that his belief is true. But generally speaking, the mere fact that someone believes something is not evidence that their belief is true. Suppose I believe that COVID-19 was created in a laboratory somewhere in China. You respond that there is absolutely no evidence for that. In reply, suppose I say, "Well, of course there is. I believe it. And that is evidence that it is true." You would not take that claim seriously, and you would be right. The mere fact that I believe something is not any evidence for it being true. Well, the same point applies to the beliefs of people who disagree with me. The mere fact that they believe differently from me is not any evidence that their beliefs are true. But then the mere fact that they disagree with me is not any reason for me to change my beliefs. Your argument has been mistakenly assuming that the mere fact that someone believes something is evidence that it is true, but that's false.

Maya: In some situations, the fact that someone believes something *is* some evidence that it is true. Think again about expert testimony. The fact that an expert believes something really is some evidence that it is true. The only reason it is absurd for you to use it as evidence in the case you mentioned is that we already know you believe it, since you already told us. So it would be redundant to say it again. But even if your belief is not evidence in that case, it is still evidence in the other cases, and I think that includes the cases that we're talking about.

Paul: That's just not obvious to me.

Maya: Okay. Here's an argument for it. Suppose that you have good reason to believe that the thermometer in your room is reliable, and it currently reads seventy-five degrees. Is that some evidence that it is seventy-five degrees in your room?

Paul: Yes, it is.

Maya: Okay. You believe that you yourself are generally reliable. Otherwise you wouldn't believe anything, since you wouldn't trust yourself. Well, if you believe that you are reliable, and you recognize that Steve is just as intelligent, thoughtful, and well informed as you are, then to be consistent you must believe that Steve is also generally reliable. Now, suppose that Steve believes something—call it X. Since you believe that Steve is generally reliable, you should also believe that someone who is generally reliable believes X. Now the situation is just like the case of the reliable thermometer. In both cases, a reliable source tells you that something is true. If you agree that it is evidence in the case of the thermometer, then you should agree that it is also evidence in the case of Steve's belief. Generally speaking, the fact that a reliable source says something is some evidence that it is true.

Steve: Yes, I see your point. You know, we have talked a lot about *trust*, and when we talked about biases, we also talked about *self-trust*. That seems relevant here. In our discussion of biases, you impressed on me the importance of self-trust in the pursuit of knowledge. If there is any knowledge to be had out there, I have to trust myself enough to think that I can get it. Since I do want to get knowledge, I think I should trust myself enough to pursue it. The risk is worth it. But if I trust myself, then when someone disagrees with me, it seems that I should continue to trust my own opinions. So here is an argument. In order to pursue knowledge, we have to trust ourselves—trust that we have the ability to achieve knowledge. If we trust ourselves, then when someone disagrees with us, and we cannot tell which of us is more reliable on the subject, then we should continue to trust our own opinion. So in such disagreements, we should continue to trust our own opinion. Otherwise, our pursuit of knowledge will simply stop.

Maya: That's an interesting argument. I agree with it up to a point, but I don't think your conclusion follows. It's true that you should trust yourself and your ability to achieve knowledge. Absolutely. But you should also trust *other people*. That was the point of our discussion of trusting experts. Knowledge depends on trusting other people, just as much as it depends on trusting yourself. So I agree that you should trust yourself, but you should also trust other people. And that is where the problem of disagreement arises.

Steve: But if I suspend judgment about my own beliefs, then my pursuit of knowledge will just stop.

Maya: No, it doesn't have to stop. You can continue to look for good evidence and arguments on the subject, and that's what the pursuit of knowledge is all about. Suspending judgment doesn't mean that you stop looking for the answer. It just means that you admit you don't know the answer yet.

Paul: Wait a minute. Something just occurred to me. This argument is self-defeating.

Steve: What do you mean?

Paul: Maya's position is that whenever two people disagree, and they cannot tell which of them is epistemically superior on the subject, they should suspend judgment about which one of them is right and which one is wrong. But now notice—people disagree about *this very subject*. I mean, the three of us are disagreeing about it right now. So if we cannot tell which of us is epistemically superior, we should all suspend judgment about the Equal Weight View, including Maya. Maya, you yourself should suspend judgment about your own view on this. Otherwise, you are being inconsistent. So you yourself cannot accept the Equal Weight View, since we disagree with you about it. So when it is applied consistently, the Equal Weight View defeats itself, doesn't it?

Maya: Well, since I am a philosophy major, I am epistemically superior to both of you on this particular subject. But there are good philosophers who disagree with me about this issue, so that won't get me out of this problem. But this objection doesn't show that the Equal Weight View is false. It only shows that, in my situation, I should suspend judgment about whether or not it's true. Even if I myself should suspend judgment about it, the Equal Weight View could still be true.

Paul: What do you mean? I don't follow you.

Maya: Right now there is disagreement about the Equal Weight View among people who seem like epistemic peers. So right now the Equal Weight View entails that I should suspend judgment about whether the Equal Weight View itself is true. You're right about that. But the Equal Weight View could still turn out to be true. At some point in the future, every thoughtful person might come to accept the Equal Weight View.

Paul: Sure, that's possible. But that doesn't help you now. Right now there is disagreement among intelligent people about whether we should accept the Equal Weight View, and thus, the Equal Weight View itself implies that we should suspend judgment about whether or not it is true. So if you accept the Equal Weight View, then in the current circumstances, you should *not* accept it, because equally intelligent people disagree with you about it. So in the end, you yourself should *not* accept the Equal Weight View.

Maya: Not so fast. There might be a way out of this problem. Perhaps some truths are so obvious that they are exempt from the Equal Weight View, and perhaps the Equal Weight View is one of those truths. Here's what I mean. Some philosophers believe in what are called *self-evident truths*. To say that a truth is self-evident is to say that if you just think about it, you can see that it is true. For example, it is self-evident that 2+2=4. If you understand what it means and you just think about it, you can see that it is true. Well, maybe self-evident truths are an exception to the Equal Weight View. If you and I are having a serious discussion, and you tell me that 2+2 does not equal 4, then I should not suspend judgment about that, even if you seem to be as intelligent and thoughtful as I am. Since it is self-evident that 2+2=4, it is not something that I should ever suspend judgment about. Well, maybe the Equal Weight View is also self-evident. It sometimes seems that way to me. If the Equal Weight View is self-evident, and if self-evident truths are an exception to the Equal Weight View, then the Equal Weight View is an exception to itself—it only applies to other truths, which are not self-evident.

Paul: That seems *ad hoc* to me. It's a case of special pleading: "Every other belief is subject to the Equal Weight View, but not that view itself."

Maya: No, I don't think so. This view doesn't make an exception for just one view. It makes an exception for an entire category of statements—those that are self-evident. So this isn't just special pleading for one particular opinion. If the Equal Weight View belongs to this group of self-evident truths, then it follows that it is an exception to the rule, but only because it belongs to this group.

Paul: That's fair enough. The special pleading doesn't occur when you make an exception for self-evident truths. The special pleading occurs when you say that the Equal Weight View is a self-evident truth. *That* is where the special pleading occurs. You think that the Equal Weight View is self-evident, but other good philosophers disagree about that. They deny that the principle is even true, not to mention self-evident. Those philosophers are in just as good a position as you to determine whether the Equal Weight View is self-evident, at least as far as you can tell. So this is just the sort of situation in which the Equal Weight View requires that you suspend judgment. Thus, you should suspend judgment about the Equal Weight View.

Maya: Hmm, I have to admit that I see your point. This defense of the Equal Weight View doesn't seem as strong as I thought it was. Now it seems like the Equal Weight View might really be self-defeating. But maybe there is a modified version of the view that is not self-defeating.

Paul: How so?

Maya: A person can have many different degrees of confidence in the truth of a belief. I hold some of my beliefs with a very high degree of confidence, and I hold other beliefs with a much lower degree of confidence. And my degree of confidence in a belief can change. Suppose I believe with great confidence that my friend will pick me up soon enough for us to get to the concert on time. As it gets later and later, and she still hasn't shown up, my degree of confidence in that belief starts to fall—it gets lower and lower. If I continued to believe, with the very same degree of confidence, that we will get to the concert on time, then that would not be rational. As it gets later, my degree of confidence in that belief should go down. Well, I'm now inclined to say the same thing about disagreement among epistemic peers. If an epistemic peer disagrees with you, then you can continue to have your belief, but your confidence in the truth of that belief should go down a bit—maybe even quite a bit. You should not remain just as confident in the truth of your belief as you were before.

Paul: Well, that view is not self-defeating. So that might be right. But it will still imply that you should not have too much confidence in the Equal Weight View itself. Since many good philosophers disagree about the Equal Weight View, you should lower your degree of confidence in it quite a bit, right?

Maya: Yes, that's true. But I can still believe it. I just have to believe it with much less confidence.

Paul: Yes, I suppose that's right.

Maya: And so I would still say that both you and Steve should have a lot less confidence in your opinions once you realize that someone who seems just as smart as you disagrees with you.

Paul: That has some plausibility. I will think about that. Maybe you're right.

Steve: I want to try out a different approach to this problem. It will take a minute to explain. Do you mind?

Maya: No, not at all.

Steve: I've been reading this book by two psychologists entitled, *The Enigma of Reason*. These two psychologists—Dan Sperber and Hugo Mercier—start with a puzzle. As we've already discussed, recent psychology seems to show that human beings are deeply and systematically biased, to the point of being very irrational. That raises a puzzle: If human reason is so deeply flawed, as it seems to be, then why did it evolve in the first place? Our brains are awfully big, and they use a lot of energy, so it would be very strange if they evolved to do something that they do very poorly. Well, these psychologists hypothesize that human reason actually works very well. To see that, you have to understand that the goal of human reason, in a single individual, is not to discover the truth but simply to persuade other people that your opinions are right. When it comes to getting other people to believe what you want them to believe, it turns out that all of those biases are very effective. You can use those biases to get people to believe what you want them to believe. And that's the point of human reason. Since we are social animals, we have to cooperate. Each individual has an interest in getting the other members of the group to cooperate on her own terms. The role of reason is to enable an individual to persuade the other members of the group to believe what you want them to believe.

Paul: This sounds like it's heading right back to the skepticism that you were considering before.

Steve: No, not this time, because now I know there's more to the story than that. I'm thinking about that study that Maya told us about, in which people reason much better when they reason collaboratively. When people reason together in groups, then they are more likely to find the right answer than when they reason alone in isolation. This is due to the fact that when someone in the group knows the right answer, they are often able to give reasons that convince the rest of the group to accept it.

Maya: Yes, that's right.

Steve: Okay. Well, let's put all of this together. When we use reason as individuals, we are not very good at discovering the truth. We are much better when we reason together in groups. So here is a hypothesis. We reason better in groups because each individual looks for the very best reasons and evidence that she can find in support of her opinion, whatever it is. If someone in the group has the right opinion, and they find good reasons for that opinion, then they give those reasons to the group, and they are often able to persuade the group. That way, the whole group, reasoning together, eventually discovers the truth.

Paul: Okay, I get the idea. But what does any of this have to do with the problem of disagreement?

Steve: Well, if these two psychologists are right, then what actually motivates us to use our reason is the desire to convince other people that we are right. That is what gets us looking around for good reasons and arguments. That is what starts this whole process of collective reasoning, which is what gives us our best chance of finding the truth. So here is a reason to hold onto your beliefs, even in the face of disagreement. You *might* be the person in the group who is right—the one who has a true belief on the subject. And if you are that person, then you need to find the evidence and the arguments that will convince the rest of us that you are right. That is the only way that we will discover the truth. But in order for you to be motivated to find those reasons and arguments for your opinion, you probably need to hold onto that opinion. Strange as it might sound, the irrational desire to convince other people that you are right is precisely what gets this process of collective reasoning started, and the process of collective reasoning is what gets us to the truth.

Paul: Yeah, I kind of like this. If that's right, then the social activity of discussion and debate is essential to our collective pursuit of knowledge. And in that process, everyone has a role to play. When we consider the role of the individual, by himself, his thoughts and behavior seem irrational, but when you see them as part of a social activity of collective reasoning, then they are actually rational.

Steve: Yes, and I think it gives each person a good reason to hang onto their beliefs, at least enough to continue looking for good evidence and arguments for those beliefs, and for presenting those reasons and arguments to the rest of us.

Maya: That's a very interesting idea. In order for the process of collective reasoning to achieve its goal, people do have to recognize good reasons when they are presented with them.

Steve: Yes, that's right. And that does mean that people should not simply ignore disagreement with intelligent peers. If they do that, then the process won't work. When intelligent peers disagree with us, we should listen to their reasons and arguments and consider them carefully. We should engage in discussion and debate with them. We should give them our best reasons for our views, and then listen to their best reasons for theirs. And we should do all of this with an open mind. If we do that, then we have the very best chance of discovering the truth, whatever it is.

Maya: That makes sense. I'll have to think about that.

Paul: You know, now that I think about it, this is relevant to another debate that Steve and I have had over the years.

Steve: Which one are you thinking of?

Paul: The debate about morality.

Steve: Ohhh, right.

Maya: So what's the debate?

Paul: I think that morality is objective. Some actions are objectively right and other actions are objectively wrong, no matter what anyone thinks about it. And I think sometimes we know which actions are objectively right and which actions are objectively wrong. But Steve disagrees, and he always points out that people disagree about morality, and that shows that it isn't really objective. Well, it now seems to me that when Steve made that argument, he was assuming something like that Equal Weight View. But now I think that we both reject the Equal Weight View, so I think he has to give up that argument.

Steve: Not so fast. I think morality is different. Moral disagreements are different from other disagreements.

Maya: How so?

Steve: Some disagreements are *factual*. They are about matters of fact. In factual disagreements, we might disagree about what the facts are, but we can at least imagine how we might discover the truth of the matter. So suppose that we disagree about some fact of history. We can imagine discovering new documents that tell us the truth of the matter. But when it comes to moral disagreements, we cannot imagine what would count as discovering "The Moral Truth." So I don't think there *is* any truth of the matter. Morality is just a matter of subjective preferences and social norms. It's purely subjective.

Paul: Well, that's your opinion, but that's where I disagree. I think that there are moral facts. It's a fact that slavery is wrong. It isn't just that some people now disapprove of it. It's really wrong. And even back when most people approved of it, it was wrong too. And the mere fact that people have disagreed about it does not show that it isn't objectively wrong.

Steve: Well, most people in the world now agree about slavery being wrong, so that makes your case seem stronger than it is. There are other moral disagreements that are not likely to be resolved. But even if they were, it would just mean that people came to share the same subjective preferences. At least, that's how it seems to me. I don't understand how there could be objective morality. That idea just seems very weird to me. I mean, where would an objective morality come from?

Maya: I know what you mean, Steve, but there are some possible answers there.

Steve: You mean that it comes from God? I know that's what Paul thinks.

Maya: Actually, that's not what I had in mind. It's an objective fact that our actions have effects on other people—specifically, some of our actions cause people to feel pleasure, and other actions cause people to feel pain. That is an objective fact. Well, what if a morally right action is just an action that causes people to feel more pleasure than pain, and a morally wrong action is just an action that causes people to feel more pain than pleasure. For any action there will be an objective fact of the matter about how much pain and pleasure it caused, and that objective fact determines whether the action is right or wrong. If that is right, then the rightness or wrongness of the action will be an objective fact. So when a sadist tortures an innocent person just for fun, that action is wrong, because it caused much more pain than pleasure.

Steve: What if the sadist really enjoys it a lot?

Maya: Look, I'm not actually defending that theory of morality. I'm just using it to illustrate one way in which morality could turn out to be objective. There are other theories of morality that would have the same result, and they don't bring God into the picture either.

Steve: Yes, I see what you mean, but those theories are just more moral assertions that people disagree about. And like I said, we cannot imagine what would constitute "discovering the truth" about which theory is correct. So I think the disagreements over morality are *intractable*—they cannot be resolved. And why would that be? I mean, if there are objective moral facts, then surely we would be able to imagine what it would be like to discover those facts. But we cannot imagine what it would be like to discover a moral fact. And I think the best explanation of that fact is that *there are no moral facts*.

Paul: Wow . . . it's almost dinnertime. Look, I want to keep talking about this, because it's something I've wondered about for a very long time. But I'm starving. What do you say we go get dinner and then meet back here to continue the conversation?

Steve: That works for me.

Maya: Me too. See you after dinner.

Chapter Five

Knowing Right and Wrong

Maya, Paul, and Steve arrive back at the room after dinner and launch right into conversation about morality.

Steve: Morality is subjective. It's just a matter of personal preference. If you believe that something is wrong, then for you it is wrong. But if someone else, in another culture, believes that it's not wrong, then for them it isn't wrong. I don't see how either person could be objectively correct about what is right and wrong.

Paul: That's how a lot of people think, but I don't think they realize what that implies.

Steve: What do you mean?

Paul: Consider this. Japan invaded China in 1937, and they started a program of extreme savagery to break the will of the Chinese people. After they took Nanking, they rounded up thousands of young men and took them out to pits, where they proceeded to use them for bayonet practice. There are photographs of Japanese soldiers stabbing Chinese men over and over again with their bayonets. Now, I'm going to go out on a limb here and say that using a living human being for bayonet practice is wrong. The victims of this torture were not even combatants. They were civilians who had been rounded up in town for no other purpose than to use their living bodies as bayonet practice. That is morally wrong.

Steve: Of course it is, and of course I agree completely. That was horrible. I don't disagree with you about that.

Paul: Yes, but given your view of morality, when you say that it was wrong, you are just saying something about your own personal preference or the moral code of your society. If they were here now, those Japanese soldiers could say, "Well, that's your preference. That's the moral code of your society. But we have a different preference and a different moral code. We prefer to use Chinese men for bayonet practice, and our moral code says that it's okay to do it." Then what could you say to that? Nothing. You have your preference and they have theirs, and that's the end of it. But see, I can't accept that. I think that what they did was wrong, *no matter what they or anyone else thought about it.* And it isn't just a matter of subjective preference or cultural norms. It's an objective fact that it was wrong.

Maya: One of my philosophy professors agrees with you. She calls that view *moral realism.* It's the view that there are objective moral truths—truths about what is right and wrong that do not depend on how anyone thinks or feels.

Paul: Yes, that's my view. I guess I'm a moral realist.

Steve: I can't accept that. I don't think anyone has the right to impose their morality on anyone else. I mean, who's to say which morality is correct? What gives me the right to tell other people how to act?

Paul: That's not what I'm saying. I'm not saying that I have the right to tell anyone else what to do.

Steve: Well, if there are objective moral truths, as you say, and if you know these objective moral truths, then shouldn't you make other people do what is objectively right?

Paul: No, I don't think that follows. I think that's a different issue.

Steve: How?

Paul: Well, I'm not sure, but I think it's different.

Maya: My professor—the one who is a moral realist—agrees with Paul here. She says that a moral realist should be tolerant of other people's opinions. And she thinks that is perfectly consistent with moral realism.

Steve: But how is it consistent? I mean, why should she be tolerant of other people's opinions if she knows the objective moral truth?

Maya: Here is what she says. If there are objective moral truths, as she believes, then no one is guaranteed to be right about them. The objectivity of morality precisely means that what is right and wrong is *independent* of anyone's opinion about it. That means that no one's opinion is guaranteed to be correct. When it comes to right and wrong, we are all fallible. My opinion on some moral issue might be correct, but it could also be incorrect. On some occasions, I might be right and believe a moral truth. I might even know that it's a moral truth. But it's always possible that I am mistaken—I don't really know it; I just *think* I do. Since that is always possible, I should be tolerant and respectful of other people's opinions on moral questions. She says that all of that is consistent with moral realism. So a moral realist should actually be tolerant of other opinions.

Steve: That sounds awfully wishy-washy to me. One minute she says that there are objective moral truths, and the next minute she says that she might be mistaken about all of them.

Maya: You can believe that there is an objective fact of the matter about something, but also believe that you could be mistaken about what that is.

Steve: How so?

Maya: Suppose I agree with the astronomer at Harvard that an extra-terrestrial UFO recently appeared in our solar system. There is some fact of the matter about this—either it was a UFO as he believes, or it was just a comet as others believe. The truth of that matter, whatever it is, is objective. And my opinion about it is that it was a UFO. But I realize that I might be mistaken. In that case, I believe all of the following things: (1) there is some objective fact of the matter about this—either it was a UFO, or it was not; (2) so either my opinion is objectively true, or the opposing opinion is objectively true—the truth of the matter is objective; and (3) my own opinion might be true, but it could also be false—I might be mistaken. Those three beliefs are perfectly consistent. My professor holds something like those three beliefs on all moral questions—questions about what is right and what is wrong. And it follows that, in her view, we are all fallible about morality, and so we should be tolerant of other people's opinions about it.

Steve: Hmm, okay. I'll have to think about that. But that just leads me to my next objection to moral realism. If there are objective moral truths, then I don't see how anyone could possibly know them.

Paul: Why not?

Steve: The problem is that people disagree about what is right and what is wrong, and I don't see how either side could ever be proven right. Give me a minute to explain this.

Paul: Sure, go ahead.

Steve: Consider *honor cultures*. An honor culture is a culture in which people—usually men—are quick to use violence to defend their honor. In an honor culture, men will respond to the slightest insult with violence.

Paul: Oh, I know what you mean. My uncle Jerry lives in Texas, and he told me that the bar down the street from him has a "No Hats" rule. The reason is that if one man knocks off another man's hat, then the second man has to fight to defend himself. Otherwise he will be seen as a coward. Well, they were having so many fights at the bar that finally they said, "No more hats."

Steve: Yes, exactly. That's a good example. There have been honor cultures throughout history, in many different places. They aren't all exactly the same, but they have some basic things in common. In an honor culture, the most important value is *prestige*. More precisely, the men in honor cultures value prestige that is achieved through contest and combat. For a man in an honor culture, achieving a high social status by beating other men in combat is the greatest good or at least part of the greatest good. That's why men in honor cultures welcome violent conflict, and sometimes even seek it out. Winning a fight and achieving honor through it constitutes a good life for a man in an honor culture.

Maya: Lovely.

Steve: I don't like it either. But my point is that people in honor cultures have a different morality from people in liberal cultures. They have different values, and they make different moral judgments. In an honor culture, if a man responds to an insult with violence, then that is seen as morally permissible as long as he did it in a fair way. In extreme honor cultures, it might even be permissible to kill a man for insulting you.

Paul: Okay, I get the idea. So how is this relevant to moral realism?

Steve: If a man responded to an insult by killing someone, then people in an honor culture would say that this was morally right, while most of the people in our culture would say that it was morally wrong. If moral realism is true, then one of us must be right and the other one must be wrong. But how could we ever discover who is right and who is wrong? How could we know? I don't see how we could. But if there is no way that we could discover who is right and who is wrong, then we cannot know who is right and who is wrong. So if there are these objective moral facts, then we cannot know them. They are unknowable. And if they are unknowable, then they are useless. They might as well not be facts at all.

Paul: Sometimes moral disagreements like this are based on the fact that people live in very different circumstances. I've read about honor cultures, and they usually exist in places where there is no central authority with enough power to enforce the law well— places like the old west in the United States. In a situation like that, where there is no one to enforce the law, it is necessary to defend your honor in order to deter people who might attack you if they think you're weak. But if that's the case, then what looks like gratuitous violence to us is really necessary for self-defense. And even our own morality permits killing in self-defense. So the apparent disagreement between our morality and their morality might not be as deep as it looks. Maybe we actually agree more than we think, and we're just living in very different circumstances.

Steve: I have heard that theory about honor cultures—that the point of the violence is deterrence, but I don't think it really explains all the facts about honor cultures. Men in honor cultures are often encouraged to attack other men in cattle raids or combat. And there is lots of evidence that people in honor cultures see contests, including violent contests, in a positive light. They see them as opportunities for men to establish themselves in the social pecking order. That isn't just about deterrence. People in honor cultures see the activity of winning prestige through violent contests as intrinsically good. The honor that is achieved in that way is what every man should aim at in those cultures. Now, that value is just fundamentally different from the values of liberal, Western societies. We have two different moralities here.

Paul: Okay, maybe so. But there are still ways in which we might discover that one of these moralities is right and the other one is wrong. Recent studies have found that in honor cultures there is more domestic violence, more child abuse, less attention to mental health issues, more reckless behavior that leads to death, and slightly higher levels of depression. So the morality of an honor culture causes more pain than our liberal morality. If people in an honor culture knew that, they might reconsider their morality.

Steve: No, I don't think they would. Your argument is based on an assumption about the importance of pleasure and pain. In our culture, we place a very high value on pleasure and the absence of pain. But that is just one more way in which our morality is different from the morality of honor cultures. A person in an honor culture would say that pleasure and pain don't matter as much as we think they do. Achieving honor in battle is a much better life than just sitting around enjoying pleasure and avoiding pain. So they would say that we are too concerned about pleasure and pain, and that prevents us from achieving truly good lives. So your argument about pleasure and pain just assumes that your liberal morality is correct. Now, how could we discover that you are right and they are wrong?

Maya: I know what you mean. Your argument is based on the apparent difference between facts and values. There are facts about how things are in the world, and then there are the ways in which we value those facts—we say that a fact is good or bad, right or wrong. Our evaluation of the fact seems like something different from the fact itself. For any fact whatsoever, we can ask whether that fact is good or bad, and that seems like a further question. The value of a fact—its goodness or badness—is not included in the fact itself. So two people can agree about the facts, but disagree about whether those facts are good or bad.

Steve: Yes, that's exactly my point. So when you say that honor cultures have more pain and less pleasure than liberal cultures, a person in an honor culture can recognize that fact but see it as irrelevant, because pain and pleasure don't have the same value in an honor culture as they have in our culture.

Paul: That's true. But sometimes people resolve their moral disagreements through reason. Over time, and through public debate, people who once disagreed often come to agree about moral issues. Think about the history of the United States over the last two centuries. In the early 1800s, most people in the United States believed that slavery is morally permissible and that women should not have the same rights as men. Over the next two centuries, there was ongoing argument and debate among people in society about those issues, and at the end of those two centuries, most people agree that slavery is wrong and that women should have the same rights as men. So moral disagreements—even very deep disagreements—often get resolved through reason.

Steve: That's true. But even back in the early 1800s, there were some fundamental moral agreements in our society. The Declaration of Independence asserted that all men are created equal, and that they all have certain rights. American society did not apply that idea consistently then, but the idea was there, and that made it possible for people to come to see that this should include people of different races and genders. But what I'm saying is that some moral disagreements are really fundamental, and that is the case in the disagreement between honor cultures and liberal cultures. We do not share the same fundamental values. Consequently, any argument for one of these two moralities will assume some value that is not shared by the other culture. So how could we ever discover which one of these two moralities is correct, and which one is incorrect?

Paul: You might be surprised. Some non-liberal societies have started to adopt liberal values. They have started to recognize individual rights, even when those rights conflict with the principles of honor cultures. And on the other side, some people in liberal societies think that honor has a legitimate place in a liberal society. So I think that we can imagine people coming to agree about morality at some point in the future.

Steve: It's certainly possible that people come to agree about morality in the future. But that does not show that they would be *discovering* the true morality. They are just changing their minds about which one to accept.

Paul: Now I think you're begging the question.

Steve: How so?

Paul: Your argument was that we could not imagine discovering that one of these moralities was right and the other was wrong. In response, I described how people could change their minds about what is right and wrong through reasoning and debate. You say that this is not a discovery, but just a change of mind. But if there are moral facts, and people come to believe them through a process of reasoning, then that would be a discovery. To deny that it would be a discovery is just to deny that there are any moral facts. But that is exactly what is at issue here— whether or not there are any moral facts. If your argument tacitly assumes that there are no moral facts, then you are just assuming what you were supposed to be proving.

Steve: Well, I guess I just don't see how we could know something like a moral fact in the first place.

Paul: Okay. Why not?

Steve: No one ever sees the rightness or wrongness of an action. If I had seen those Japanese soldiers using the Chinese men for bayonet practice, I would have seen what the soldiers looked like, how they thrust their bayonets, and where they entered the victims' bodies, but I wouldn't have seen the *wrongness* of their actions. Where was that? If I were to write down everything I saw with my eyes, I would describe what the men looked like, how they moved, and so on, but I would not write: "Oh, and I saw the *wrongness* of their actions too." That wouldn't make any sense. No one ever sees the rightness or wrongness of an action, and they don't hear it or taste it or smell it or feel it either. No one perceives objective rightness or wrongness with their senses. So how could you know the objective rightness or wrongness of an action?

Paul: Really? Why can't you just see that an action is wrong?

Steve: Well, consider this. Imagine a Japanese soldier who saw the bayonet practice, just like I did. They saw everything that happened, just as well as I did. They would deny that the action was wrong. And in denying that the action was wrong, they wouldn't be contradicting anything they saw. They just make a different moral judgment about it. They evaluate the action differently.

Paul: Okay, yes, I see what you mean. We don't perceive rightness and wrongness with our senses. So if objective rightness and wrongness exist, then they are things that we cannot perceive with our senses. So what? Why can't there be things that are not perceived with our senses?

Steve: I don't deny that there *could be* things we can't perceive with our senses, but until we see something or perceive it with one of our senses, we have no reason to believe in it, and no way to know that it's real. That's why I don't believe in fairies. I've never seen one. If you have never perceived something with your senses, then you have no reason to believe it's real.

Paul: So you only believe in what you can perceive with your senses?

Steve: Yes, that's right.

Maya: Steve's view is a very strict type of *empiricism*. Empiricists believe that all of our knowledge comes through our senses. The only way that you can really know something about the world is by perceiving it with one of your senses.

Steve: Yes, that's what I think. So I guess I'm an empiricist.

Paul: But you do trust science, right?

Steve: Absolutely. Science is based on observation, and that's exactly how I think we should form all our beliefs—through observation with our senses.

Paul: But then here's a problem. Science tells us that there are lots of things that we cannot perceive with our senses—things like atoms and molecules.

Steve: Actually, you *can* see atoms and molecules. You just have to use an electron microscope.

Paul: That's true. But what about *quarks?* Quantum physics tells us that quarks exist, and that they compose protons and neutrons.

But you cannot see a quark—not even with an electron micro-scope. So no one has ever seen a quark. So there are things that we cannot see. Isn't that right?

Steve: Not so fast. I'm not sure that we should accept the existence of quarks. When physicists first suggested that atoms existed, there were some physicists who refused to accept the existence of atoms until atoms were actually observed. Only after atoms were actually observed did they accept that atoms exist. I think those physicists were right, and I think we should take the same atti-tude toward quarks. Since we haven't observed them, we should not believe that they exist.

Paul: But if quarks are what physicists say they are, then it is physically impossible to observe them, so we will *never* observe them. If we stick to your standard, then we will never accept the existence of quarks, even though physics tells us they exist.

Steve: Yes, that's true. And now that I think about it, I don't think we should ever accept their existence.

Paul: But then you're rejecting science.

Steve: No, hear me out. Quantum physics is a successful theory insofar as it makes accurate predictions, and I think that's what that the-ory is for. It's good science because it makes accurate predictions. But that doesn't mean that we have to accept it as literally true. It's useful for the purpose of making accurate predictions, and that's all we want from it.

Maya: I understand where you're coming from, Steve, but I think you're being too cautious. Let's think about the case of atoms again. We had good evidence for the existence of atoms even before any-one actually observed them, and we have good evidence for the existence of quarks now. That is because both quarks and atoms *explain* a whole bunch of things that we *do* observe. Our belief in atoms and quarks is based on an *inference to the best explanation*.

Steve: What do you mean by that?

Maya: The greatest discoveries in the history of science have all been made through inference to the best explanation. First we observe something in nature, and we wonder why it happens. We ask: "What causes this to happen?" Then someone thinks of a possible explanation. At first, this is just a hypothesis—a hypothesis that, if it were true, would explain why we observe what we observe. Then we ask if the truth of this hypothesis would explain what we observe better than any other hypothesis that we can think of. If it does give us the best explanation, then we infer that this hypothesis is probably true. This has happened over and over again in the history of science. Newton observed that physical bodies move in certain ways, and he wondered why. At some point it occurred to him that if there were a certain kind of force—the force of gravity, then that would explain why things move in the way they do. So he formed a hypothesis— that there exists a force of gravity that acts on all physical bodies. That hypothesis turned out to explain all the motions of all physical bodies, and so scientists gradually came to accept that the hypothesis is true.

Steve: Okay, sure. He got that one right.

Maya: Well, the same thing happened with infectious diseases in the late seventeenth century. People noticed that some diseases are infectious—they pass from person to person. But no one really knew how this happened. Have you seen pictures of the creepy masks that doctors used to wear during the plague?

Steve: The ones that looked like bird beaks?

Maya: Yes, exactly. Well, they wore those masks because they didn't understand how the plague was transmitted—they thought that it was due to poisonous air. Well, in the late seventeenth century, some scientists hypothesized that infectious diseases are actually caused by microscopic entities of some sort—things too small to see with the naked eye. Of course, that turned out to be true—we now know that bacteria and viruses cause infectious diseases.

Steve: Yes, that's true.

Maya: And atoms and quarks were discovered in the same way. Physicists hypothesized that if these things existed, then that would explain what we observe. When the explanations succeeded, then they came to accept that the hypotheses were true. In each of these cases, scientists reasoned in the same way. They used *inference to the best explanation*. And in many of these cases, the best explanation involved things that had not been observed through our senses yet. Before we could see gravity or bacteria or atoms or quarks, we had good reason to believe that they existed, because their existence gave the best explanation of what we did observe.

Steve: Yes, that's true. But in all of those cases, we eventually observed those things. We can now *see* bacteria and viruses under a microscope. We can *see* atoms with an electron microscope. And we can actually feel the force of gravity. We can perceive all of those things with our senses, at least with the use of instruments like microscopes and electron microscopes. That is why we have good reason to believe in those things. But quarks are different. We can't see them, and we never will. Since we can't see them, and we never will, I think we should not infer that they really exist.

Maya: But all those other discoveries demonstrate that inference to the best explanation *works*—it's a reliable method. If someone in the seventeenth century had used inference to the best explanation to infer the existence of bacteria and viruses, without ever observing them, they would have known that bacteria and viruses existed. They didn't need to observe them to have good reason to believe that they were real. And the same goes for atoms. Although we eventually observed them, we didn't need to observe them in order to know that they exist. Think about it: Why would anyone have built instruments to observe those things if they didn't have good reason to believe that they existed? Here is one more example to illustrate the point. After Newton discovered his laws of motion, many people noticed that the orbit of the planet Uranus was not quite what Newton's laws said it should be. The orbit was just a little bit off. In 1846, the French astronomer Urbain Le Verrier hypothesized that there was another planet just beyond Uranus, and that planet was causing the orbit that we observed. Le Verrier was using inference to the best explanation. If there was another planet located in that place, then that would explain Uranus's orbit. Of course, when astronomers looked for the planet, sure enough, they saw it. It's the planet Neptune. But Le Verrier had good reason to believe that Neptune existed even before it was observed, because Neptune's existence gave the best explanation of what we observed. In general, if the truth of some hypothesis gives us the best explanation of what we observe, then we have good reason to believe that the hypothesis is true. And that's how we know that quarks exist. Their existence gives us the best explanation of many observations that we make.

Steve: I see your point. Look, when it comes to things that are observable, at least in principle, then I accept inference to the best explanation. But you want to use it to infer the existence of things that are unobservable, and that's where I disagree.

Maya: But why should that make a difference? Inference to the best explanation worked for bacteria and viruses and molecules and atoms, even when we had not yet observed them, and that gives us good reason to trust it when it comes to unobservable things like quarks.

Steve: But again—bacteria and viruses and molecules and atoms were all things that *could be observed* at some point. Quarks are literally unobservable in principle. That seems like a relevant difference to me.

Maya: Well, consider this anecdote from history. When Galileo started making discoveries with a telescope, some people asked why they should trust the telescope. To answer the question, Galileo used the following strategy. He asked them to use the telescope to look at a building one hundred yards away. They could then walk over to that building and use their own senses to confirm what they had seen through the telescope. Then he had them do the same thing at 200 yards, and 300 yards. Then Galileo argued like this: if the telescope is reliable at 100 yards and at 200 yards and at 300 yards, then why would it not be reliable at even greater distances? If the telescope proves to be reliable at every distance at which you can confirm its reliability, then why would it not be reliable at greater distances too? I think Galileo was right, and the same point applies to inference to the best explanation. It has proven reliable in those cases in which we can test its results with our senses, and that is good reason to trust it even when we cannot test the results with our senses, as with quarks.

Steve: Maybe that's right. Maybe I should accept inference to the best explanation, and believe in quarks, even though they are unobservable. But how is that relevant to moral rightness and wrongness? Rightness and wrongness aren't quarks, after all.

Paul: You were arguing that we should only believe in things that we can perceive with our senses, and since we cannot perceive objective rightness or wrongness with our senses, we should not believe in them. My reply was that science itself gives us good reason to believe in unobservable things. As Maya explained, science is based on inference to the best explanation, and inference to the best explanation sometimes gives us reason to believe in things that we cannot observe, like quarks. So science itself tells us that there are things that are unobservable by us. So the mere fact that objective rightness and wrongness are unobservable is not a good reason to deny that they exist.

Steve: Well, we have good reason to believe in quarks, because they give us the best explanation of things that we observe with our senses. So in order for us to have reason to believe in objective rightness and wrongness, it would have to be true that objective rightness and wrongness give us the best explanation of things that we observe with our senses. But they don't. Rightness and wrongness don't explain anything.

Paul: Not so fast. Moral rightness and wrongness might explain some of the things that happen in the world. Specifically, moral qualities might explain why some people act the way they do. Why did Martin Luther King Jr. risk his life and sacrifice his life, to lead a movement for Civil Rights? He did it because *it was the right thing to do.* And there are other examples of that too. Sometimes I go visit an elderly relative, even though I don't feel like doing it, because I know it's the right thing to do. The correct explanation of these actions is that people did them because they were the right things to do.

Steve: Well, you certainly *could* explain those actions in that way, but inference to the best explanation requires that this explanation be *the best* explanation of what we observe. But there are other explanations of these actions that are just as good or even better, and they don't involve any objective rightness or wrongness. Martin Luther King acted in the way he did because he *believed* that it was the right thing to do. And you went to visit your elderly relative because you *believed* that it was the right thing to do. In such cases, we can explain why people acted the way they did just by referring to their *beliefs* about right and wrong. We don't need any real rightness or wrongness to explain how people act. We can explain it just by reference to their moral beliefs. Consider this analogy. Imagine a seventeenth century Puritan who believes that his neighbor is a witch. He avoids her and speaks ill of her and eventually reports her to the authorities. He does all these things because he believes that she is a witch.

His belief explains his behavior. We don't have to accept that his neighbor is really a witch in order to explain his behavior. His *belief* that she is a witch is enough to explain his behavior.

Paul: I'm shocked that you are denying the existence of witches. I think I need to report this to someone.

Steve: Very funny. Look, sometimes people act a certain way because they *believe* that it's morally right to act that way. And sometimes people protest and rebel because they *believe* that a certain law or policy is unjust. In all these cases, we can explain people's behavior by reference to their moral *beliefs*. We don't need anything to be really right or wrong for this explanation. So there is no inference to the best explanation for moral rightness and wrongness.

Paul: Okay, but why do people have those moral beliefs? Isn't it because some actions really are morally right, and other actions really are morally wrong? If so, then we will still need rightness and wrongness to explain something that we observe—people's moral beliefs.

Steve: I don't think we need real rightness or wrongness to explain people's moral beliefs either.

Paul: What do you mean?

Steve: I think that evolutionary biology can explain where morality came from. Morality evolved because it was conducive to the survival and reproduction of our species. Our ancestors' moral values helped them survive and reproduce better than their competitors, and that's why we have the moral values that we have.

Paul: How could morality be conducive to survival and reproduction? Morality requires you to care about other people and to make sacrifices for them—for your brothers and sisters, friends and neighbors, and even complete strangers. How could making sacrifices to help other people help me to survive and reproduce?

Steve: There are a few different ways to explain how morality could contribute to survival and reproduction. Here is the one that seems the most plausible to me. At some point in our evolutionary history, our ancestors had opportunities to cooperate with each other. Those who cooperated effectively were able to survive and reproduce better than those who did not cooperate effectively. So being able to cooperate with other humans was conducive to survival and reproduction. At some point, some of our ancestors began to feel *empathy* for other people. Of course, empathy motivates helping behavior. When you empathize with another person, then you are inclined to help them. Some of our ancestors empathized with other human beings and helped them. At this stage of our evolution, human beings were forming coalitions for the purpose of cooperation. People who empathized with others and helped others acquired a reputation for being good coalition members. If you were looking for someone to join your group, then an empathetic person was just the sort of person you would want. You could count on them to help you.

Paul: Yeah, but they can also be a real buzz kill.

Steve: I'll pretend you didn't say that. Look, the point is that those with empathy gained a reputation for being good coalition partners, and that gained them entry into the best coalitions. The best coalitions were the most effective at cooperating, and so every member of the coalition would have a better rate of survival and reproduction. The moral of the story is that morality evolved because it promoted social cohesion and cooperation. All of our moral beliefs and attitudes resulted from the fact that those beliefs and attitudes have held human societies together, and enabled them to cooperate in ways that led to our survival and reproduction.

Paul: That's an interesting story, but it's all pretty speculative.

Steve: Yes, it is somewhat speculative. But remember Maya's point— science is often based in inference to the best explanation. I think that something like this hypothesis is probably true because it explains where our moral beliefs and attitudes came from, and it explains it in a way that is consistent with everything else that evolutionary biology tells us about ourselves.

Paul: Well, even if that's true, it doesn't really contradict moral realism, does it?

Steve: If this hypothesis is true, then it poses a real problem for moral realism.

Paul: How so?

Steve: Morality evolved because it facilitated social cohesion and cooperation and for that purpose, no one needed to discover any objective moral truths. All that was needed was a set of moral beliefs or attitudes that produce the right behavior—social cohesion and cooperation. Any set of moral beliefs that achieves that would evolve, as our morality did.

Paul: But it is still possible that this evolutionary process led to the discovery of objective moral truths. Isn't that possible?

Steve: Sure. It's possible that evolution led to the discovery of objective moral truths, but it isn't likely.

Paul: Why not?

Steve: It would be an incredible coincidence. Consider an analogy. Suppose that I give you the following task: you need to create a myth for a group of people—a myth that the entire group will believe wholeheartedly. The sole purpose of this myth is to get these people to form social groups and cooperate. That is the sole purpose of the myth. Now, if that is your only purpose, then does it matter whether the myth is true or not? No. When you sit down to write your myth, you will only focus on one issue: What myth would be the most effective in getting people to form social bonds and cooperate? If you do your job well, then that is all you will think about. You won't worry about whether the myth is true or not, because that has nothing to do with the purpose of the myth. And in that situation, is it likely that you will write a myth that just happens to be objectively true? No, it isn't likely at all. Well, according to my hypothesis, morality is just like that—it's a myth that was designed to achieve social cohesion and cooperation. It's just that in this case, the myth was not written by a person, but by the process of evolution by natural selection.

Paul: I have some doubts about this argument. Look, natural science is also the product of evolution, in some sense. The cognitive abilities that eventually led to natural science were produced by evolution. But then, by your reasoning, natural science is not discovering any objective truths. But that isn't right. So there must be something wrong with your argument.

Steve: Sense perception evolved because it gives us knowledge of the environment around us. You cannot explain the evolution of sense perception unless you see it as giving us knowledge of the outside world. And the same goes for the other cognitive abilities that eventually led to natural science. They evolved because they give us knowledge of the world around us. But our best theory of the evolution of morality does *not* say that it evolved because it gave us knowledge of objective moral truths. Our best theory says that morality evolved for another purpose—one that has nothing to do with moral truth.

Paul: Okay, but how do we know that the process of evolution was the only force that played a role in the development of morality? What about culture? What about reason? Didn't they also play a role in the development of morality? And might those explain how we eventually discovered moral truths?

Steve: I think the best explanation of morality is that reason and culture are just the channels through which human evolution now expresses itself. When you look at our morality, it is just what you would expect if it were produced solely by human evolution. So I think that our best overall explanation of morality is that human evolution alone produced it, and reason and culture are just the ways in which we now express our evolutionary inheritance. Reason and culture are just the effects of human evolution, and when it comes to morality, they don't significantly change the way in which we have evolved.

Paul: Maya, what do you think about this? You haven't said much.

Maya: Well, I'm just very happy to see you guys having such a great conversation without yelling at each other, so I didn't want to stop you. But since you asked, I'm happy to tell you what I think. To be honest, this is something that I'm still thinking about, and I'm not really sure that I have a settled opinion yet. But there is one possible view that is different from either of your views, and I think you should consider it. Suppose that Steve's hypothesis is right—morality evolved because it promoted social cohesion and cooperation. Steve assumes that the goal of promoting social cohesion and cooperation is a different goal from the goal of discovering any objective moral truth. But maybe these aren't really separate goals at all.

Steve: I don't understand. Promoting social cohesion and cooperation doesn't require discovering any objective truth. That's the point of the analogy with creating a myth.

Maya: Yes, I understand that. But this all depends on the nature of *moral truth*, which is something that we haven't really talked about. It depends on what is required for a moral statement to be true or false. Here is what I mean. We sometimes help other people because we see that they are in trouble and they need help. We empathize with them, and our empathy leads us to help them, even if there is nothing in it for us. In cases like this, our actions are caused by empathy, which is the very sentiment that led our species to cooperate, to form societies, and to become the human beings that we are today. This pattern of feeling and acting is what made us who we are. Well, what if that very fact *makes it true* that such actions are morally right? Maybe moral truth just consists in being true to this aspect of our nature as human beings—our capacity to empathize with other human beings and to act on that empathy in ways that benefit them, even if it doesn't always benefit us.

Paul: Well, I certainly agree that acting in that way is often morally right, but I think that the fact that it is right has to be based on something more than just the fact that we evolved in this way. I mean, what if we had evolved differently? Then would moral truth be different from what it is? Would empathy and altruism be morally wrong? And suppose someone says: "I don't care about how we evolved. I don't care that empathy played a crucial role in the evolution of humanity. I think we should overcome all of that. We should become something more than human." Is it now right for him to act cruelly?

Maya: Those are all great questions, and we should talk about them. As I say, I haven't really made up my mind about this yet. Next semester I am taking a seminar on this subject, which is called "metaethics." It's all about whether morality is subjective or objective. Well, right now I really have to study, so I'm going to have to quit for now. But before I go, I want to say one more thing to both of you, if that's okay.

Paul: Absolutely.

Steve: Of course, go ahead.

Maya: Our evolutionary history tells us a lot about ourselves as human beings, and one of the things it tells us is that we are social animals by nature. We survived because we cooperated. I think that the future of humanity depends on our ability to continue to cooperate and to do it better. But our differences constantly threaten to tear us apart. In order to prevent that, we have to keep talking to each other. We have to maintain a respectful dialogue, even in the face of deep disagreements. We have to keep talking to each other and keep listening to each other, so that we can learn from each other. That's what we need to do if we want to survive and thrive. So I hope that we keep talking to each other and listening to each other, even when we disagree.

Paul: Is it time to sing "Kumbaya" around the campfire now?

Steve: You are impossible!

Maya smiles as she leaves the room.

Notes

CHAPTER ONE: WHERE ARE THE EXPERTS?: Paul's story about the development of his autistic brother is inspired by the story of Cindy Pokezwinski, as recounted in her editorial, "MMR vaccine caused my son's autism," published in the *Deseret News* on May 23, 2013. The idea that vaccines cause autism was first inferred from a study by Andrew Wakefield, published in the *Lancet* in 1998. That study has since been discredited and Wakefield has been accused of fraud. The *British Medical Journal* published a series of three articles in 2010 and 2011 detailing all the facts of the case. A study of over 500,000 children in Denmark found that there was no connection between the MMR vaccine and autism. The study was published in the *New England Journal of Medicine* in 2002. Alice Stewart's survey of children who had died of cancer, which found a correlation with prenatal X-rays, was also published in the *Lancet* in 1956: "Preliminary Communication: Malignant Disease in Childhood and Diagnostic Irradiation *In Utero*" (*The Lancet*, 1956). For the details of the case, see G. Green, *The Woman Who Knew Too Much: Alice Stewart and the Secrets of Radiation* (University of Michigan Press, 1999). The problem of knowing who the experts are is discussed at length in Alvin Goldman's article, "Experts: Which Ones Should You Trust?" (*Philosophy and Phenomenological Research*, 2001). The study that initiated the so-called replication crisis in psychology was "Estimating the Reproducibility of Psychological Science" (*Science*, 2015). The idea that knowledge depends on trust is defended by John Hardwig in two articles: "Epistemic Dependence" (*Journal of Philosophy*, 1985); and "The Role of Trust in Knowledge" (*Journal of Philosophy*, 1991). The position that testimony is innocent until proven guilty was defended by the Scottish philosopher, Thomas Reid (*Inquiry into the Human Mind: On the Principles of Common Sense*, 1764). A version of that view is also defended by C. A. J. Coady (*Testimony: A Philosophical Study*, Oxford University Press, 1992). The opposing view—that the rationality of trusting testimony depends on independent evidence that it is reliable—was defended by the Scottish philosopher, David Hume (*An Enquiry Concerning Human Understanding*, 1748). A version of this view is also defended by Elizabeth Fricker in "The Epistemology of Testimony" (*Proceedings of the Aristotelian Society*, 1987). The view that it is rational for people to trust the traditions in which they were raised, even when alleged experts contradict those traditions, is defended by Theodore Everett in "The Rationality of Science and the Rationality of Faith" (*Journal of Philosophy*, 2001).

CHAPTER TWO: THEY'RE ALL BIASED!: The facts cited about the political affiliation of many college faculties are reported in "Faculty Voter Registration in Economics, History, Journalism, Law and Psychology" (*Econ Journal Watch*, 2016). The neuroscientific study of what happens in people's brains when their political beliefs are challenged is reported in "Neural Correlates of Maintaining One's Political Beliefs in the Face of Counterevidence" (*Scientific Reports*, 2016). An excellent overview of the psychological research on cognitive biases is Cordelia Fine's book, *A Mind of Its Own: How Your Brain Distorts and Deceives* (W. W. Norton, 2005). Another excellent book on the subject is *Nudge: Improving Decisions about Health, Wealth and Happiness*, by Richard Thaler and Cass Sunstein (Yale University Press, 2008). There is evidence that confirmation bias is the chief cause of wrongful convictions: see "'Confirmation Bias' Called a Key Reason for Wrongful Convictions" in *The Crime Report*, July 16, 2019. The use of bias attributions to "debunk" the opinions of others is discussed in Nathan Ballantyne's essay, "Debunking Biased Thinkers (Including Ourselves)" (*Journal of the American Philosophical Association*, 2015). Maya's position on this issue is a version of Ballantyne's in that essay. The Dream Argument is due to the great French philosopher René Descartes, in his *Meditations on First Philosophy* (1640). The indispensability of self-trust for the pursuit of knowledge is defended at length by Richard Foley in *Intellectual Trust in Oneself and Others* (Cambridge University Press, 2001).

CHAPTER THREE: I READ IT ON THE INTERNET: My discussion of the epistemology of the internet is deeply indebted to Michael Lynch's excellent book, *The Internet of Us: Knowing More and Understanding Less in the Age of Big Data* (Liveright Publishing, 2016). The Afghanistan papers are summarized in "At War with the Truth," by Craig Whitlock (*Washington Post*, December 19, 2019). The idea that knowledge is true belief produced by intellectual virtues was developed and defended by Ernest Sosa in a long series of books and articles. See his collection of essays, *A Virtue Epistemology: Apt Belief and Reflective Knowledge*, Vol. 1 (Oxford University Press, 2007). Hugo Mercier and his colleagues found that collective reasoning is more reliable than solitary reasoning and reported their findings in "Arguments, More than Confidence, Explain the Good Performance of Reasoning Groups" (*Journal of Experimental Psychology*, 2014). My discussion of conspiracy theories draws heavily on David Coady's excellent article, "Conspiracy Theories and Official Stories" (*International Journal of Applied Philosophy*, 2003). Paul's initial argument in defense of conspiracy theories is drawn from Lance deHaven-Smith, in *Conspiracy Theory in America* (University of Texas Press, 2014).

CHAPTER FOUR: WE STILL DISAGREE: David Christensen and Jennifer Lackey defend the Equal Weight View in "Epistemology of Disagreement: The Good News" (*Philosophical Review*, 2007). Peter van Inwagen appeals to private, incommunicable insights in "It Is Wrong, Everywhere, Always, and for Anyone, to Believe Anything upon Insufficient Evidence" (*Faith, Freedom, and Rationality*, Rowman and Littlefield, 1996). Thomas Kelly has argued that beliefs are not evidence in the way required by the Equal Weight View in "The Epistemic Significance of Disagreement" (*Oxford Studies in Epistemology*, Vol. 1, 2005). The problem of self-defeat for the Equal Weight View is discussed by Adam Elga in "How to Disagree about How to Disagree" (in *Disagreement*, edited by Richard Feldman and Ted Warfield, Oxford University Press, 2010). The idea that the Equal Weight View is exempt from itself because it is obviously true is defended by Tomas Bogardus in "A Vindication of the Equal Weight View" (*Episteme: A Journal of Social Epistemology*, 2009). The thesis that the function of human reason, in individuals, is to persuade others to accept our views is supported by Hugo Mercier and Dan Sperber in *The Enigma of Reason* (Harvard University Press, 2017).

CHAPTER FIVE: KNOWING RIGHT AND WRONG: To see the photographs of Japanese soldiers using Chinese men for bayonet practice, go to: https://www.pacificwar.org.au/JapWarCrimes/Cross-section_JapWarCrimes.html. Steve's interpretation of honor cultures is developed by Dan Demetriou in "What Should Realists Say about Honor Cultures?" (*Ethical Theory and Moral Practice*, 2014). The many adverse effects of honor cultures are described by Ryan Brown, in *Honor Bound: How a Cultural Ideal Has Shaped the American Psyche* (Oxford University Press, 2016). The thesis that we should not believe in quarks because they are unobservable is derived from the work of Bas van Fraassen: *The Scientific Image* (Oxford University Press, 1980); and *Quantum Mechanics: An Empiricist View* (Oxford University Press, 1991). Galileo's strategy for demonstrating the reliability of the telescope and its relevance to scientific realism is discussed at length by Philip Kitcher in "Real Realism: The Galilean Strategy" (*Philosophical Review*, 2001). Gilbert Harman argued that moral claims cannot be tested by observation in *The Nature of Morality* (Oxford University Press, 1977). The idea that moral facts provide the best explanation of moral beliefs has been defended, to some extent, by Don Loeb in "Moral Explanations of Moral Beliefs" (*Philosophy and Phenomenological Research*, 2005). Steve's evolutionary explanation of the origins of morality is developed and defended by

Philip Kitcher in *The Ethical Project* (Harvard University Press, 2014). The argument that such explanations undermine moral realism is defended by Sharon Street in "A Darwinian Dilemma for Realist Theories of Value" (*Philosophical Studies*, 2006). The response that facts about social cohesion and cooperation might actually constitute moral truth is developed by David Copp in "Darwinian Skepticism about Moral Realism" (*Philosophical Issues*, 2008).

Bibliography

Ballantyne, Nathan. "Debunking Biased Thinkers (Including Ourselves)." *Journal of the American Philosophical Association* 1 (2015): 141–62.

———. *Knowing Our Limits*. Oxford: Oxford University Press, 2019.

Bogardus, Tomas. "A Vindication of the Equal Weight View." *Episteme: A Journal of Social Epistemology* 6 (2009): 324–35.

Brown, Ryan. *Honor Bound: How a Cultural Ideal Has Shaped the American Psyche.* New York: Oxford University Press, 2016.

Christensen, David. "Epistemology of Disagreement: The Good News." *Philosophical Review* 116 (2007): 187–217.

Christensen, David, and Jennifer Lackey. *The Epistemology of Disagreement: New Essays.* New York: Oxford, 2013.

Coady, C. A. J. *Testimony: A Philosophical Study.* Oxford: Oxford University Press, 1992.

Coady, David. "Are Conspiracy Theorists Irrational?" *Episteme* 4 (2007): 193–204.

———. "Conspiracy Theories and Official Stories." *International Journal of Applied Philosophy* 17 (2003): 197–209.

———, ed. *Conspiracy Theories: The Philosophical Debate.* New York: Ashgate Publishing Company, 2006.

Coady, David, and James Chase. *The Routledge Handbook of Applied Epistemology.* London: Routledge, 2019.

Copp, David. "Darwinian Skepticism about Moral Realism." *Philosophical Issues* 18 (2008): 186–206.

deHaven-Smith, Lance. *Conspiracy Theory in America.* Austin: University of Texas Press, 2014.

Demetriou, Dan. "What Should Realists Say about Honor Cultures?" *Ethical Theory and Moral Practice* 17 (2014): 893–911.

Descartes, René. *Meditations on First Philosophy.* Translated by Donald A. Cress. Indianapolis: Hackett Publishing Company, 1993.

Elga, Adam. "How to Disagree about How to Disagree." In *Disagreement*, edited by Richard Feldman and Ted Warfield, 175–86. Oxford: Oxford University Press, 2010.

Enoch, David. "Not Just a Truthometer: Taking Oneself Seriously (but not Too Seriously) in Cases of Peer Disagreement." *Mind* 119 (2010): 953–97.

Everett, Theodore. "The Rationality of Science and the Rationality of Faith." *Journal of Philosophy* 98 (2001): 19–42.

Feldman, Richard, and Ted Warfield. *Disagreement*. Oxford: Oxford University Press, 2010.

Fine, Cordelia. *A Mind of Its Own: How Your Brain Distorts and Deceives*. New York: W. W. Norton, 2005.

Foley, Richard. *Intellectual Trust in Oneself and Others*. Cambridge: Cambridge University Press, 2001.

Frances, Bryan. *Disagreement*. Cambridge: Polity Press, 2014.

Fricker, Elizabeth. "The Epistemology of Testimony." *Proceedings of the Aristotelian Society*, Supplementary Volume (1987): 57–83.

Godlee, Fiona, et al. "Wakefield's Article Linking MMR Vaccine and Autism Was Fraudulent." *British Medical Journal* 342 (2011): 7452.

Goldberg, Sanford. *Relying on Others: An Essay in Epistemology*. Oxford: Oxford University Press, 2010.

Goldman, Alvin. "Experts: Which Ones Should You Trust?" *Philosophy and Phenomenological Research* 63 (2001): 85–110.

Green, G. *The Woman Who Knew Too Much: Alice Stewart and the Secrets of Radiation*. Ann Arbor: University of Michigan Press, 1999.

Hardwig, John. "Epistemic Dependence." *Journal of Philosophy* 82 (1985): 335–49.

———. "The Role of Trust in Knowledge." *Journal of Philosophy* 88 (1991): 693–708.

Harman, Gilbert. *The Nature of Morality*. Oxford: Oxford University Press, 1977.

Hume, David. *An Enquiry Concerning Human Understanding* (1748). Indianapolis: Hackett Publishing Company, 1993.

Jamieson, Kathleen Hall, and Frank Capella. *Echo Chamber: Rush Limbaugh and the Conservative Media Establishment*. Oxford: Oxford University Press, 2008.

Kaplan, Jonas T, Sarah I. Gimbel, and Sam Harris. "Neural Correlates of Maintaining One's Political Beliefs in the Face of Counterevidence." *Scientific Reports* 6 (2016).

Kelly, Thomas. "The Epistemic Significance of Disagreement." In *Oxford Studies in Epistemology*, Vol. 1, edited by Tamar Szabo Gendler and John Hawthorne, 167–97. New York: Oxford University Press, 2005.

Kitcher, Philip. *The Ethical Project*. Cambridge, MA: Harvard University Press 2014.

———. "Real Realism: The Galilean Strategy." *Philosophical Review* 110 (2001): 151–97.

Lackey, Jennifer. *Learning from Words*. Oxford: Oxford University Press, 2008.

———. "What Should We Do When We Disagree?" In *Oxford Studies in Epistemology*, edited by Tamar Szabo Gendler and John Hawthorne. Oxford: Oxford University Press, 2010.

Lackey, Jennifer, and Ernest Sosa, eds. *The Epistemology of Testimony*. Oxford: Oxford University Press, 2006.

Langbert, Mitchell, Anthony J. Quain, and Daniel B. Klein. "Faculty Voter Registration in Economics, History, Journalism, Law and Psychology." *Econ Journal Watch* 13 (2016), 422–51.

Loeb, Don. "Moral Explanations of Moral Beliefs." *Philosophy and Phenomenological Research* 70 (2005): 193–208.

Lynch, Michael. *The Internet of Us: Knowing More and Understanding Less in the Age of Big Data*. New York: Liveright Publishing, 2016.

Madsen, Kreesten Meldgaard, et al. "A Population-Based Study of Measles, Mumps and Rubella Vaccination and Autism." *New England Journal of Medicine* 347 (2002): 1477–82.

Mercier, Hugo, and Dan Sperber. *The Enigma of Reason*. Cambridge, MA: Harvard University Press, 2017.

Millgram, Elijah. *The Great Endarkenment*. Oxford: Oxford University Press, 2015.

Nguyen, C. Thi. "Echo Chambers and Epistemic Bubbles." *Episteme* 17 (2020): 141–61.

Nosek, Brian, et al. "Estimating the Reproducibility of Psychological Science." *Science*, August 28, 2015.

Oreskes, Naomi. *Why Trust Science?* Princeton: Princeton University Press, 2019.

Pariser, Eli. *The Filter Bubble: How the New Personalized Web Is Changing What We Read and How We Think*. London: The Penguin Press, 2011.

Pokezwinski, Cindy. "MMR vaccine caused my son's autism," *Desert News*, May 23, 2013.

Reid, Thomas. *Inquiry into the Human Mind: On the Principles of Common Sense* (1764). In *Thomas Reid's Inquiry and Essays*, edited by Ronald Beanblossom and Keith Lehrer. Indianapolis: Hackett Publishing Company, 1983.

Saul, Jennifer. "Skepticism and Implicit Bias." *Disputatio* 5 (2012): 243–63.

Selinger, Evan, and Robert Crease, eds. *The Philosophy of Expertise*. New York: Columbia University Press, 2006.

Shieber, Joseph. *Testimony: A Philosophical Introduction*. New York: Routledge, 2015.

Sosa, Ernest. *A Virtue Epistemology: Apt Belief and Reflective Knowledge*, Vol. 1. Oxford: Oxford University Press, 2007.

Stewart, Alice. "Preliminary Communication: Malignant Disease in Childhood and Diagnostic Irradiation *In Utero*." *The Lancet* 268, no. 6940 (September 1956): 447, https://doi.org/10.1016/S0140-6736(56)91923-7.

Street, Sharon. "A Darwinian Dilemma for Realist Theories of Value," *Philosophical Studies* 127 (2006): 109–66.

Sunstein, Cass. *#Republic: Divided Democracy in the Age of Social Media*. Princeton: Princeton University Press, 2017.

Thaler, Richard, and Cass Sunstein. *Nudge: Improving Decisions about Health, Wealth and Happiness*. New Haven: Yale University Press, 2008.

The Crime Report. "'Confirmation Bias' Called a Key Reason for Wrongful Convictions." July 16, 2019. https://thecrimereport.org/2019/07/16/confirmation-bias-called-a-key-reason-for-wrongful-convictions/.

Trouche, E., E. Sander, and H. Mercier. "Arguments, More than Confidence, Explain the Good Performance of Reasoning Groups." *Journal of Experimental Psychology* 143 (2014): 1958–71.

Van Fraassen, Bas. *Quantum Mechanics: An Empiricist View*. Oxford: Oxford University Press, 1991.

———. *The Scientific Image*. Oxford: Oxford University Press, 1980.

Van Inwagen, Peter. "It Is Wrong, Everywhere, Always, and for Anyone, to Believe Anything upon Insufficient Evidence." In *Faith, Freedom, and Rationality*, edited by Jeff Jordan and Daniel Howard-Snyder. London: Rowman & Littlefield Publishers, 1996.

Wakefield, Andrew, et al. "Ileal-Lymphoid-Nodular Hyperplasia, Non-Specific Colitis, and Pervasive Developmental Disorder in Children." *Lancet* 351 (1998): 637–41.

Walton, D. *Appeal to Expert Opinion*. University Park: Pennsylvania State Press, 1997.

Watson, Jamie Carlin. *Expertise: A Philosophical Introduction*. London: Bloomsbury Academic, 2020.

Whitlock, Craig. "At War with the Truth." *Washington Post*, December 19, 2019.

Index

Afghanistan, 53, 71–72, 122
altruism, 119; and cooperation, 115–19
Aristotle, 26, 74
autism, and vaccines, 1–5, 121, 126

belief, 7–8, 30–34, 38–50, 55–62,
    71–72, 77–88, 91–94, 101, 108,
    113–16
bias, 5, 7, 26-52, 75-82, 88-93, 122;
    anchoring bias, 39–41; attribution
    of, 34–38; 121, availability bias,
    40–41; bias blind spot, 35–36;
    confirmation bias, 38–41, 49, 122;
    political bias, 29–34, 122; self-
    serving bias, 31; and skepticism,
    41–52
Borges, Jorge Luis, 54

circular argument, 11–12
classism, 58
consistent, consistency, 18, 31, 37, 48,
    82, 87–89, 100–101, 105, 116
conspiracy theory, 5, 51–53, 58, 65–76,
    122–23; definition of, 65–67;
    and naiveté, 72–74; and paranoia,
    68–74; rationality of, 65–75
contradiction, 32–33
Copernicus, Nicolaus, 25
credentials, 10–11

degrees of confidence, 91–92
disagreement, 75–105; between
    epistemic peers, 75–95; and
    experience 83–86, moral, 95–105
Dream Argument, 44–48
dreams, 44–48; dreaming and
    skepticism, 44–48

echo chambers, 60–62
empathy, 115–19; and altruism,
    115–19; evolution of, 115–18

empiricism, 107; and morality, 107–13;
    and quantum physics, 107–13
epistemic bubble, 59–62
epistemic peers, 77–95; definition of,
    77; frequency of, 79–80
Equal Weight View, 81–82
error, 46–50; possibility of, 46–47
evidence, 4, 8–10, 14–25, 30–32, 35,
    38–39, 46, 49, 51, 55, 60–62, 68–70,
    72, 76, 87–88, 93-94; absence of
    evidence vs evidence of absence, 4
evolution, 114–19; of morality, 114–19
experience, 2, 14, 19–24, 32, 45, 83–86;
    incommunicability of, 83–86
experts, expertise, 1–27, 31–33, 81–82,
    87–88, 121
explanation, 12, 67–71, 97, 108–17;
    inference to the best, 108–12

fallible, fallibility, 15–17, 100–101
falsehood, 50–54
framing bias, 40

Galilei, Galileo, 25, 112, 123
group-think, 12–13, 29, 40
gullible, gullibility, 6, 13, 19

hallucination, 15
Holmes, Sherlock, 57
honor cultures, 101–5, 123

intellectual vice, 56–59, 71–74
intellectual virtue, 56–59
internet, 53–65, 122; and democracy,
    5–59; and misinformation, 53–65

King, Martin Luther, Jr., 113
knowledge, 13–18, 49–50, 55–60, 88,
    107, 117, 121; as non-accidentally
    true belief, 55–58: basic source of,
    13–18; conditions for, 55–60

129